Kavitha Mandana is the author of eight books for children published by Puffin (Penguin), Karadi Tales, Pratham and Red Turtle (Rupa). Her short fiction has appeared in various anthologies as well as in school English textbooks. She's been writing and illustrating for the *Deccan Herald*'s kids' supplement for the past twenty years.

The Emperor Who Vanished

Strange Facts from Indian History

KAVITHA MANDANA

TALKING CUB
Published by Speaking Tiger Publishing Pvt. Ltd
4381/4 Ansari Road, Daryaganj,
New Delhi–110002, India

First published in paperback in Talking Cub by
Speaking Tiger 2018
Copyright © Kavitha Mandana 2018
Inside illustrations by Kavitha Mandana

ISBN: 978-93-88326-37-7
eISBN: 978-93-88070-10-2

10 9 8 7 6 5 4 3 2 1

The moral right of the author has been asserted.

Typeset in Cardo by Jojy Philip
Printed at Gopsons Papers Ltd.

All rights reserved.
No part of this publication may be reproduced,
transmitted, or stored in a retrieval system, in any form
or by any means, electronic, mechanical, photocopying,
recording or otherwise, without the prior permission
of the publisher.

This book is sold subject to the condition that it shall not,
by way of trade or otherwise, be lent, resold, hired out,
or otherwise circulated, without the publisher's
prior consent, in any form of binding or cover
other than that in which it is published.

The Emperor
Who Vanished

Strange Facts from Indian History

Chapter 1

Apu and Nina sat across each other at a table in the library, in silence. They both had a dictionary open in front of them. Nina said, worriedly, 'You're right, I guess. It says here that "rusticate" means to suspend from school or college.'

'Sssshhhhhh,' hissed the librarian from her desk behind the 'books for kindergarten' section.

Apu stuck out his tongue and whispered, 'I told you so…and you thought Mathur Sir wanted us to learn about "rustic life"! Ha! What a joke!'

Nina pretended not to care, but she so hated being proved wrong, by Apu in particular. Yet, she still found it difficult to believe anyone would want to 'rusticate' them—they, the team that had just won the 'Best Social Studies Model' prize. And only because silly Apu knocked over and broke that very same model. Didn't being rated 'Best' count for anything? Even if that 'Best' was now broken?

She said, 'I wish I wasn't always paired with you for Social Science projects. It's just my luck that both our surnames begin with R.'

'You're acting as if this is my fault. It was your brilliant idea to make a "real" river model for the project,' Apu hissed, careful not to attract the librarian's wrath.

'Yes, but it was you who clumsily knocked over our model and sloshed all that water across the room, ruining Sir's brand new shoes.'

'But if we hadn't had real water in our model, Sir's shoes wouldn't have got ruined when the model broke…I hope you realize that it's ruined shoes that's landed us here, and not a broken model,' Apu lashed out, almost forgetting to keep his voice low.

Resigned to their fate, the two put away the dictionaries and reluctantly settled down to some long hours of boring Social Studies research. Neither of them wanted to be suspended, so if Mathur Sir insisted on forty pages of research on the 'Ancient Structures of India', Nina and Apu decided they'd give him fifty pages, just to be safe.

They began with the Taj Mahal, certain they couldn't go wrong there. Apu swore that he'd follow all of Sir's rules. Only relevant information, Sir had cautioned, well aware of how these two tiring children tended to go chasing information that was 'out of proportion', 'unnecessary' or 'simply useless'. All Sir wanted were the measurements, the materials used and which king built which structure.

Nina grumbled, 'He'll make us collect all this boring stuff and give us these facts itself for "Fill in the Blanks" in our next test. Pah!'

They'd searched for and got down all the boring details about the Taj, when Nina spotted a little box in the encyclopaedia she'd opened. It was something about Delhi and Agra being in a seismically active zone. That was enough to set off the two fact-finding bloodhounds on a merry chase. Before they knew it, their half-page of boring facts on the Taj Mahal was dwarfed by the three pages they wrote on what Sir was JUST NOT INTERESTED IN!

The Taj Mahal is located in a high seismic zone, yet it has never been damaged by an earthquake

What is a 'high seismic zone'?

The regions around Delhi and Agra in north India are in an earthquake-prone belt. On a scale where Zone 1 is considered safe and Zone 5 dangerous, Delhi and Agra are in Zone 4.

A number of massive earthquakes have struck the north of India and indeed the entire Himalayan belt over the centuries. In 1935, Quetta, now part of Pakistan, was hit by a huge earthquake. It flattened the city and killed over 10,000 people. At the eastern end of the Himalayan fault line, Assam has been hit by big earthquakes, most notably in 1897 and 1950, killing thousands.

In the century preceding the building of the Taj Mahal, a series of devastating earthquakes occurred across the Himalayan fault line. It began with a quake in Kashmir, in 1501. One month later, an earthquake hit what is today's Afghanistan. And in 1505, in the central Himalayas, another devastating earthquake hit. This could be felt within a radius of 500 miles from the epicentre. It destroyed monasteries in Tibet, north of the Himalayas, and tremors were felt as far south as Agra. This quake was so violent, it wiped out 30 per cent of Nepal's population. Then decades later, the year before a teenaged Akbar became king, in 1555, Kashmir was rocked by another quake.

So how exactly has the Taj survived three and a half centuries without damage in the seismically active Zone 4?

What could have preserved the Taj?

Since historians haven't quite agreed 100 per cent on who the architect of the Taj Mahal was, and because there are no architectural drawings of this great monument, we can only guess at how the monument has stood unshaken over the years.

The Emperor Who Vanished

For instance, historians do know that the four minarets have been specifically designed to lean away from the main structure. Soaring a majestic 138 feet each, the minarets have been built up from an octagonal base, and taper towards the top, where an eight-windowed chhatri is perched. There are winding stairs up to the top of each minaret (that are now closed to the public). Each minaret is off plumb (or off centre) to different extents, ranging from leaning 2 inches outwards, to 8 inches away. So if ever the tremors from earthquakes in the region get strong, causing the minarets to fall—they'd fall *away* from the Taj, not damaging it in any way.

In Islamic architecture, the dome is considered the most perfect of earthly structures. But in a seismically active region, a large dome would also be the first to collapse, being the only part of the structure with its centre (also the highest point) not supported from below.

Shah Jahan, the reigning Mughal emperor, wished to build the Taj Mahal as a tribute to his beautiful wife Mumtaz Mahal. And so, to build the Taj's famous dome, he hired Ismail Afandi from Turkey. He was known across the region as an expert dome-builder and designer of hemispheres. He was already well regarded by the Ottoman rulers of Turkey. This choice would have been crucial to the Taj's longevity. Afandi came from a region that is (in) famous for devastating earthquakes that occur in tragic regularity. In 1268, Turkey had witnessed a quake in Anatolia that killed 60,000—a disaster that was recorded and lamented for centuries. In 1509, a quake in Istanbul killed over 10,000. And in Afandi's own lifetime there were two deadly quakes in Turkey, in 1667 and 1668. So Turkish builders, in particular, had developed considerable expertise in building quake-resistant monuments.

Of the thirty-seven members of Shah Jahan's core team comprising engineers, turret builders, marble workers, etc. nearly all came from regions which regularly witnessed earthquakes—Persia, Syria, Afghanistan, Turkey, etc. So it is probable that apart from the sheer beauty of the Taj, a key element of its design is that it is earthquake-proof to a certain extent.

Picture-perfect

There's another reason that the minarets slant away from the main structure. Shah Jahan was a perfectionist. And how this monument that was a tribute to his wife looked, was very important to him. The main viewing point to gaze upon the monument is the simple marble bench that most tourists take selfies from. From that point, if the minarets were at perfectly perpendicular positions, they would *appear* as though they were leaning *towards* the Taj, which would be jarring—and hence the slight off-plumb position.

Chapter 2

Having written about one Indian monument, with half-a-page of statistics for Sir and loads of interesting titbits for themselves, Nina and Apu felt they'd struck gold.

'At this rate, we'll be done soon…within weeks rather than months,' Nina said hopefully, 'Sir will be happy, and he need never know about all our "unnecessary" research.'

But Apu wasn't listening to her. His nose was in an illustrated book about Delhi's famous but mysterious iron pillar. Nina decided to stay out of Apu's way—for now, at least. She quietly collected the height-weight details about the iron pillar, and somehow stretched all that data to cover almost two pages.

Once that was done, she peered over Apu's shoulder and read what he'd got.

Has the Iron Pillar near the Qutub Minar really never rusted?

What do palaeographists have to do with iron pillars?

For over 200 years, historians, palaeographists and translators have argued over the main Sanskrit inscription on the Iron Pillar standing at the Qutub Minar complex in Delhi.

Palaeography is the study of ancient inscriptions, languages and manuscripts. This does not involve the *meaning* of the text as much as *dating it*. So while a Sanskrit pandit might translate the inscription correctly, a palaeographist will step in and say something like,

'These words were borrowed from Greek, so it means this Sanskrit inscription can only have been from after Alexander's arrival in India in 326 BCE.' So words, styles of language usage, the evolving grammar, references to historical events, are all clues that paleographists use to date inscriptions and manuscripts.

The translation of the Sanskrit inscription on the Iron Pillar reads:

He on whose arm fame was inscribed by the sword, when in battle with the Vanga countries, he kneaded (and turned) back with (his) breast the enemies who, uniting together, came against (him); he by whom, having crossed in warfare the seven mouths of the (river) Sindhu, the Vahlikas were conquered; he, by the breezes of whose prowess the southern ocean is even still perfumed.

He, the remnant of the great zeal of whose energy, which utterly destroyed (his) enemies like (the remnant of the great glowing heat) of burnt-out earth; though he, the king, as if wearied, has quitted this earth and has gone to the other world, moving in (bodily) form to the land (of paradise) won by the merit of his actions but remaining on this earth by the memory of his fame.

By him, the king who attained sole supreme sovereignty

*in the world acquired by his own arm and (enjoyed) for a
very long time; (and) and who having the name of Chandra,
carried a beauty of countenance like the beauty of the full
moon, having in faith fixed his mind upon (the god) Vishnu,
this lofty standard of the divine Vishnu was set up on the hill
(called) Vishnupada.**

Who built the pillar?

Contrary to what guides at the Qutub Complex often
say, this is not a victory pillar but a 'dhwaja stambha' or
flagstaff, originally installed at a Vishnu temple. Since
the inscription mentions that the king who installed the
pillar was a Vishnu devotee, that straightaway disqualifies
the Mauryan Chandragupta, who was a Jain.

Palaeographists believe the script belongs to the
Gupta era (320 CE to 495 CE). The confusion arises
because the Gupta dynasty had too many 'Chandras'—
there's Chandragupta I; then his son Samudragupta
(who was also known as Chandraprakasha) and finally
the latter's son, Chandragupta II.

---

*   From *The Iron Pillar at Delhi* by Professor T.R. Anantharaman,
UBS Publishers and Distributors Ltd

Some historians believe that it was Samudragupta (Chandraprakasha) who installed the pillar at a Vishnu temple, and after his death, his son Chandragupta II had the pillar inscribed with verses praising his father. The exploits mentioned tie in with Samudragupta who was the best general from this dynasty—he crossed the Indus ('seven mouths of the Sindhu') to defeat the Balkhs, conquered Bengal (Vanga) and many parts of south India. Other historians argue that it was Chandragupta II who put up the pillar, and after his death his son Kumaragupta had the many verses praising his father inscribed on the pillar.

How has the iron not rusted over 1,600 years?

That's the other big riddle about the Iron Pillar (apart from who created it). Metallurgists from all over the world have studied the pillar and subjected it to many tests over the last 100 years.

In 1961, just before the centenary of the Archaeological Survey of India, the pillar was removed from where it stood within the Qutub complex, studied, chemically cleaned and reinstalled it. Studies conducted at this stage showed that only those parts of the pillar that were *not* exposed to the air had rusted. On top of the capital of the pillar, there was a fairly deep groove, probably into which the flag post fitted in. But in the absence of the pole, water, dust and other impurities had collected in it and caused just that groove to rust. Before reinstalling the pillar, this groove was cleaned and sealed. Parts of the pillar that were buried under the ground also showed signs of rusting. But the entire 7-metre length of the pillar above the ground that's exposed to the atmosphere (apart from the groove on the top) showed virtually no signs of rust—even after about 1,600 years!

Over the last thirty years, metallurgists have analyzed the composition of the iron used. They found that the iron has an unusually high content of phosphorous (0.1 per cent) and slag, while having less sulphur and manganese content. The phosphorous content reacts with the seasonal cycles of wind and moisture and over time becomes iron hydrogen phosphate hydrate, which forms a passive (non-rusting) thin coating on the pillar, preventing further rusting. This is why the surfaces exposed to the air haven't rusted, but the buried part has.

How was such a tall pillar constructed?

In 1989, the ultrasonic pulse-echo method (non-destructive testing) was used to study the pillar by scientists of the National Physical Laboratory, Delhi. This confirmed what earlier studies had reported, that there were high variations in the pillar's composition across its different parts. This proved that the pillar had not been made by melting the iron and casting it in one long mould. Rather, it had been built up gradually, by hammer-forging successive additions of 20-30 kg lumps of hot iron sponge. Welding lines and impressions of the hammer can be clearly seen on the pillar. This technique was well known even during Gupta times, and was used over subsequent centuries by Adivasi metal-workers who lived in central India and other regions where high iron content allowed surface mining.

And where is the pillar from?

This argument has not been settled. Because the pillar is a Vishnu flagstaff, some historians believe that it was transported to Delhi from Mathura, a pilgrimage centre important to Vishnu devotees, which is fairly close to Delhi. Others believe that the pillar originally stood at Udayagiri, a spot that ties in better with the inscription ('...hill called Vishnupada'), because here, there are hills, compared to Mathura which is plain. Also, Udayagiri is in that part of central India that had rich deposits of iron ore.

The other completely baffling question is who transported this pillar from the Vishnu temple by the hills to its present location? Truly, this Iron Pillar is shrouded in mystery!

Sorry, hugging in public not allowed!

Studies in the 1990s showed that it takes about three years for the protective, passive layer of iron hydrogen phosphate hydrate to form. By the 90s, the habit of tourists wrapping their arms around the pillar had led to an orange discolouration at that height, suggesting that rust was forming at that level. This was because the protective coating was getting worn off by constant human contact. Once a metal fence was put up around the pillar and people could no longer touch it, the iron hydrogen phosphate hydrate layer formed again, and the discolouration around the pillar vanished.

Chapter 3

'Not just monuments, but ancient cities too have so many strange facts hidden in their history,' said Nina, after leafing through a book on Pataliputra.

'Sir told us to focus on monuments...But I guess we could find that stuff anywhere. What's this about Pataliputra?' Apu leaned over to take the book from her.

'It's amazing! Pataliputra was a megacity of ancient India. But do you know that it completely vanished from all records?'

Apu looked intrigued. So they decided to postpone 'copying from the text' for information about monuments and dived into Pataliputra's past, looking for clues on how an entire city vanished.

How did Pataliputra, a megacity of its time, vanish completely?

How do you trace a once-glorious city, when it leaves almost no traces on the ground, but lives on in fables, myth, historical and travel writing? Well, archaeologists can be called in and they can start digging...wasn't that how the Indus Valley cities were discovered? But the site of Pataliputra, close to present-day Patna, seemed to offer very little evidence by way of archaeological evidence such as walls, pottery and coins.

The glory days

Over a period of about 800 years, Pataliputra, on the banks of the River Ganga had grown into a megapolis. It was the capital city for the Haryanka dynasty, whose well-known kings were Bimbisara (not to be confused

The Emperor Who Vanished

with Bindusara, Ashoka's father) and Ajatashatru. Later the Nandas took over. The first Mauryan king, Chandragupta made it his capital. By the time his grandson Ashoka ruled India (268-232 BCE), Pataliputra was one of the world's biggest and most prosperous cities.

After the Mauryan dynasty fell, the Shungas ruled from the city. Pataliputra became a boom town all over again under the Guptas, who ruled from this capital till about 550 CE.

But by the late 7th century, the city was in ruins, with no trace of its glory days. And unlike Delhi, a capital city that has seen many dynasties rule and fall, Pataliputra dropped off the map.

It was under Emperor Ashoka, a well-known Buddhist, that Pataliputra reached its peak. So historians looked for clues of this famous capital in his other Buddhist projects, like the great Sanchi Stupa, 900 kilometres west of this once-great city. It's from the tableaus carved on the walls of the Sanchi structures that you can begin to visualize what Pataliputra once was. That, combined with reports written by the Chinese and the Greek visitors, help bring the city back to life.

Since Buddhism had spread to China, Tibet and Sri

Lanka, pilgrims from these countries visiting Bodhgaya and Sanchi also checked out Pataliputra. Fa-Hsien, who came to India during the reign of Chandragupta II (380-415 CE), wrote about a city that was rich beyond description.

Can a whole city shift on the map?

No, but a river's course can. Two thousand years ago, Pataliputra was on the banks of the River Ganga. Over the centuries, the river's course has changed, shifting miles away from its original path. The city had grown rich mainly because of its location on the map. It was positioned where the rivers Son and Saryu joined the Ganga. So in the days when roads were scarce and railways didn't exist, river trade was most efficient. Wharfs along the city's northern wall jutted into the river where goods were loaded and unloaded. The city had a population of about 400,000 in Ashoka's time, so food from the entire Gangetic plain arrived at the wharfs.

But 200 years after Fa-Hsien wrote his travelogue, when Hsuan Tsang visited in 637 CE, the city was in ruins. And even after excavations at the site, we can only speculate about what caused such a booming metropolis to collapse.

The Huns, a Central Asian tribe, did invade northern India around 455-67 CE, when Skandagupta, the last of the Gupta empire, was on the throne. Though there is no record of the Huns attacking Pataliputra, their intimidating presence in the areas that the city traded with would have killed commerce. And with the river trade dwindling and the wharfs empty, the city would not have been able to support itself, however strong its fortifications.

Another possible cause for the city's destruction was its location, so close to the river. In 575 CE, the Ganga had one of its worst floods, so that could have wiped out centuries of hard work and also a large portion of the population. Excavations also show evidence of a great fire.

The first dig

In 1913, the Archaeological Survey of India (ASI) began digging outside Patna. In fact, this dig was partly sponsored by Sir Ratanji Tata, the son of Jamsetji Tata, the founder of the Tata group of industries. His first cheque of Rs 15,000 was quite a fortune over a hundred years ago, and allowed the ASI to hire 1,300 labourers for the dig. During the course of this excavation, Jamsetji's son donated another Rs 75,000 to unearth the secrets of this famous city.

One important finding (at what is now known as the Kumhrar site) during this dig—led by D.B. Spooner from the British ASI—was a 72-pillared hall. Speculations range from it being Ashoka's darbar hall to a venue built specifically for a big Buddhist conference. They also found remains of a hospital and parts of a fort wall—all pieces of a large jigsaw puzzle that will probably take years to assemble.

In the 1950s, an excavation by the Patna-based K.P. Jayaswal Research Institute unearthed eight more stone pillars, after which this is referred to as the '80-pillared hall'. But due to continuous water seepage into the excavated site, the ASI re-covered it in sand and soil in 2014, hoping to prevent deterioration of the black-spotted buff sandstone monolithic pillars. Currently, the ASI is studying ways to prevent water seepage, so that it can again be opened to the public.

A Greek temple for a Greek bride?

Greek records are full of details about the city—it was 16 km x 3.5 km, surrounded by a massive 40-km wooden wall. Chandragupta Maurya later strengthened these walls with stone and earth. Its streets were well laid out, with separate quarters assigned for different trade guilds. There were facilities for travellers, for the sick, the poor and even an animal hospital that Ashoka set up. There were many Greeks living in the city and since the Mauryan kings were very liberal, there was even a Greek temple for them to worship at, apart from Buddhist viharas, Jain and Hindu temples.

When Alexander reached the north west of India, his battle-weary army won a few minor skirmishes in areas now in Pakistan. But reports of the Nanda rulers' military strength demoralised his troops. So Alexander was forced to return to Greece.

His general, Seleucus Nicator, stayed back to govern the newly conquered lands in Iran and Afghanistan. He decided to invade India after Alexander died and attacked what was now a Mauryan army, led by Chandragupta. But the Greeks were defeated badly and had to give up a lot of territory to the Mauryas. To make peace, Seleucus sent Chandragupta a bride, believed to be his daughter, along with Greek artists and artisans. It's their accounts in Greek that tell us what the city was like.

Chapter 4

Apu and Nina were sitting at opposite corners of the library. They'd just quarrelled badly, all in whispers of course. Apu had come up with the idea of researching step wells. Nina thought it was a waste of time.

'You know, all Sir is interested in are kings, dynasties and wars…and yes, heights and weights. He'll just look at this and say "totally useless".'

But Apu sulked, 'So we won't show it to him…I think if we do a topic that doesn't interest Sir once in a while, it's okay. We don't have to show it to him.'

Secretly, Nina agreed with Apu, but the more they went chasing information Sir didn't want, the longer they would be stuck with each other in the library. She decided to leave Apu alone and quickly looked up facts on the largest dome in India. Later Apu showed her what he'd written up about step wells.

India had one of the best water harvesting systems in the world

Over centuries, in the driest parts of India, people adapted to their harsh life in different ways. One of the most brilliant and beautiful solutions to tackling low rainfall and extreme heat is the step well—called 'vav' in Gujarat; 'baoli' in Delhi; 'bawri' or 'bawdi' in Rajasthan; and 'bavi' in Karnataka.

Who built them?

Many of these structures were built by queens, rich women, kings and other patrons, for public use. The same care and expense that went into building a temple or a palace went into building a step well. While palaces soared many metres upwards, step wells went many storeys *downwards*. In Rajasthan's Chand bawdi in Abineri village 95 kilometres out of Jaipur, you can climb *down* thirteen storeys, going 30 metres into the ground, to fetch water during the dry summer. This beautiful structure was built between 800 CE and 900 CE, begun by King Chanda of the Nilkumbh dynasty. So it is clear that over 1,200 years ago, our ancestors living in the driest parts of India, understood how precious water was, and went to great pains to conserve it.

The recently restored Agrasen ki Baoli in New Delhi at Hailey's Road, Connaught Place, goes down 60 metres. And two more step wells have been restored in the Mehrauli Heritage Park in Delhi.

These step wells have ornate colonnades, balconies, landings and niches where idols are worshipped. On hot, dry days the temperature next to the water, approximately 20 metres down, would be 5–6 degrees cooler. The step well served many purposes. With the water often shielded from direct sunlight, evaporation during summer would have been low compared to big open tanks like the 76-acre Kankeriya tank in Ahmedabad, built by Ahmad Shah in 1451 CE. With so many wide landings, shrines and balconies on the multiple storeys of a step well, women who collected water during the scorching summers of Rajasthan, Gujarat, Delhi or north Karnataka, must have also met their friends and worshipped their gods here.

Waiting to be restored

Gujarat, with its arid climate, has a number of step wells. Yet, strangely, many of these were abandoned and unused over the centuries. In a country where the monsoons often fail, it is strange that the elaborate rainwater harvesting channels, inlets and sluices of step wells and open reservoirs were allowed to get overgrown, silted up or disrupted for some reason. The Solanki dynasty, which ruled Gujarat through parts of the 10th and 11th centuries CE, had mastered the art of water storage and hydraulics. In the famous Rani ki vav, in Ahmedabad, there are many Solanki era sculptures.

After the Solankis, when the Muslim kings ruled Gujarat, they too adopted this ancient practice and went about building step wells. The Bai Harira vav (also known as the Dhai Harir vav, which later got corrupted to Dada Harir vav) goes down an impressive 70 metres. It was built in 1499, by a woman with the same name, who according to different accounts, is either believed to have been an advisor to the king, Mahmud Begra or the superintendent of the harem. This was built close to the Bai Harira mosque. This is a rare case of the step well having a fairly impressive entrance. Usually, the entrances are very simple, with the architecture and sculptures getting more ornate as you climb down the stairs.

The Pushkarni or Kalyani in Hampi, Karnataka, has elaborate geometric steps going down. This open step well is a great tourist attraction. But barely 95 kilometres away, in Lakkundi in Gadag district, are a series of beautiful step wells, sadly all in disrepair. The most visited is the Muskina Bavi (the veiled well) attached to the Manikeshvara temple, the Kanna Bavi and the Chatteer Bavi. This region is extremely dry and arid, so recently, borewells have been dug in areas surrounding these bavis. This has led to the water table dropping dramatically, so even deep step wells are no longer filling up during the rains.

Since these structures have stood for centuries, isn't it strange that no new step wells are being built, and nor are the old ones maintained well?

Charles Correa's tribute to the vanishing step well

Charles Correa (1930–2015) was one of India's greatest modern architects. He built great structures by combining the best of India's ancient knowledge about weather, local materials and affordability. His unique artistic vision was recognized across the world.

When he was invited by the Rajasthan government to design the Jawahar Kala Kendra at Jaipur, he got a chance to pay tribute to the desert state's water conservation history. He designed the central courtyard like a Rajasthani kund or step well…maybe as a nudge to state authorities to revive this great building art.

Chapter 5

By the time Apu was done with step wells, Nina finished what had caught her interest—the whispering gallery in the Gol Gumbaz of Bijapur in Karnataka.

Apu read it and much to her surprise, said, 'This is the one write-up that will keep both us and Sir happy. It's got all that we're interested in AND Sir's silly measurements!'

Did architects create whispering galleries by accident, or were they planned?

A case of digging your own grave

Much like the Egyptian Pharaohs, who lived 3,000 to 4,000 years before them, the Adil Shahi rulers of the

Bijapur Sultanate (1489–1686) in present-day north Karnataka, also believed in grand tombs. Mohammed Adil Shah (like his father, Ibrahim Adil Shah) was quite obsessed with building his own mausoleum. Mohammed was just sixteen years old when his father died in 1627 and was buried in a beautiful tomb called the Ibrahim Rauza, in Bijapur, which had been ready well in time. So Mohammed also decided not to waste time. Midway through his thirty-year reign, he began work on his own mausoleum, which he'd planned on an ambitious scale. This is what we now know as the Gol Gumbaz in Bijapur.

The tiny details of this massive structure

The Gol Gumbaz has one of the largest domes in the world. When it was built over a period of about fifteen years, nothing like it had been attempted in India. Mohammed Adil Shah died in 1656, and his tomb was not quite complete—at least not the decorative elements. Thankfully, the core was solid because this structurally path-breaking building has survived centuries.

To support a dome 90-odd feet high required a very strong base. Hence a massive square hall was built.

The four walls, each 135 feet long, rose to a height of 100 feet, and were 9 feet thick. From the ground to the top of the dome is 198 feet.

At the point where the dome begins, there is a wide whispering gallery that runs along the base of the dome. The acoustics here are sensational. Anything whispered at one end of the gallery can be heard clearly on the opposite side of the gallery, over 40 feet away. This is because the sound doesn't travel across the room, but along the curved surface of the dome's wall. Four seven-storeyed towers at the four corners of the massive hall have staircases going up to the whispering gallery.

But obsessed as he was about his tomb, Mohammed Shah hadn't started work early enough. When he died in 1656, his mausoleum wasn't quite ready. The massive hall was done, and thankfully the dome built, but the plastering of the dome was still going on. No one knows whether the Gol Gumbaz as we see it today is the complete structure planned by the king or did some parts get left out because he died?

Whispering galleries

For tourists, the whispering gallery is the main draw, but architects do not set out to design such galleries. Many curved surfaces, even in open-air gardens can work like whispering galleries. The high wall around the Temple of Heaven in Beijing (built in the 1400s), carries whispers across great distances, out in the open. But the Gol Gumbaz is certainly the largest whispering gallery in the world. Its dome itself is the second largest unsupported structure, after St Peter's in Rome.

Another famous whispering gallery is in St Paul's cathedral in London. Here too, when architect Christopher Wren designed the building, the acoustics was not on his mind. He set out to build the most elegant dome that would dominate the London skyline. Only when it came up in 1669 (a decade or so after the Gol Gumbaz) did visitors who climbed up the 257 steps to the first gallery discover the whispering aspects of the building. Sadly, history has not recorded who the architect of the Gol Gumbaz was. So we'll never know if sound was part of his plan, or whether he was as surprised as Sir Christopher that his visually stunning dome also had great acoustics.

The Emperor Who Vanished

When cathedrals turn into labs for Nobel laureates

In the 1870s, physicist Lord Rayleigh (John William Strutt) studied the acoustics beneath the St Paul's dome thoroughly, conducting a series of experiments there. He was the first one to propose the idea of sound travelling in a curvi-linear path, along curved surfaces. His book *The Theory of Sound* is still a reference for acoustic engineers more than a century later. Lord Rayleigh won the Nobel Prize in 1904.

In 1921, C.V. Raman and a colleague climbed up the 257 steps to the whispering gallery at St Paul's and conducted their own experiments. Later that year, Raman visited Calcutta and wrote a paper about whispering galleries of the East. Though he mentioned the Gol Gumbaz, he confessed that he hadn't been there, yet. His studies on sound were conducted at the Victoria Memorial in Calcutta, the Calcutta General Post Office and the Bankipore granary, that had been abandoned for decades on account of a faulty design.

While the Victoria Memorial had been known to visitors

as a whispering gallery, the acoustic properties of the post office and the granary were Raman's discoveries! Raman went on to win the Nobel Prize in 1930, for the Raman Effect, his studies on light. But his visits to the whispering galleries do reveal that he was also interested in sound.

Chapter 6

Apu and Nina were hungry. As the week-long Social Science festival was ending, the school had organized some food stalls run by volunteers. But Apu and Nina were imprisoned in the library instead. They decided not to waste time grumbling about all that they were missing out on and quickly settled on a famous Rajput fort. The plan was to just collect its height, number of gates, the battles it withstood, the number of times it changed hands between princely families, etc. Apu had even drawn up a table, into which Sir's much loved statistics could be quickly filled in.

But then they saw a picture of a haveli in Shekhawat, Rajasthan. And suddenly, that fort and the royal families looked boring. Instead Nina and Apu wasted a whole hour on painted family homes, which they both knew would irritate Sir.

Isn't it strange that the largest collection of frescoed houses in the world lies in India?

And even stranger is that most Indians have no idea about this!

Fresco is the technique of painting directly onto the wall or ceiling of a building, while the plaster is still wet. In that way, the lime (as in 'chunna') plaster and the pigments from the paint chemically react to bond as one layer and when they dry simultaneously, they can last for centuries. It's a practice that began along the Mediterranean countries. We know that frescoes were painted even 1,500 years before Christ, by the Minoans of Crete and by the Greeks. Fine samples exist from excavations at Pompeii, where the volcanic ash of Mount Vesuvius has preserved the art well.

An Indian flavour to European art

But you don't need to travel that far to see a good fresco. India has some wonderful examples and this art form has bloomed in the most unlikely of places—in the Rajasthan desert! Unlike much of ancient Indian art, the frescoes of Shekhawat are not purely religious in nature. Here you can see Lord Krishna cavorting with the gopikas, right next to a panel of a steam engine! Battle scenes are painted next to love scenes. And Hanuman has been painted driving a car, with Rama and Sita in the back seat.

No royals around, for a change

Normally, such large-scale art production required the patronage of maharajas and emperors. But these beautiful frescos adorn the innumerable old houses or havelis of the Marwari community that originated from the Shekhawat region of Rajasthan. The region falls within the triangle of Delhi, Jaipur and Bikaner. If you pull out a detailed map of India, you can look for towns like Mandawa, Fatehpur, Ramgarh, Parasrampura, Mukundgarh, Bissau, Khetri and Navalgarh—all of which boast of lovely old painted havelis.

This is the region from where 'seths' migrated to other parts of India. Family names that are now associated with some of India's big business houses originated here. Frescoes adorn virtually every surface of the Goenka haveli, the Poddar haveli and the Chaudhri haveli. In the eighteenth, nineteenth and twentieth centuries, as families migrated out of this desert land and built their fortunes elsewhere, they sent back funds to develop their grand family homes. Hundreds of these courtyard houses cropped up in the desert landscape, each of them covered both on the inside and outside with colourful frescoes.

For a period of over 200 years, the art of the painted houses was popular. The fashion supported a thriving population of 'chiteras' (painters) and 'chajeras' (masons). In the 1800s, when the Shekhawati mansion-building boom was at its peak, getting enough chiteras proved difficult. So the chajeras stepped up and took on that task. They worked in teams and covered small patches of a wall or roof surface at a time. This is because the entire cycle of lime-plastering, drawing and colouring had to be finished within a short period of time—before the plaster dried. Women and young boys ground the lime and mixed it with water and curd to make the plaster. The chajeras plastered the walls, after which drawings were quickly traced onto this wet surface, and the colour pigments added to blend with the plaster. When the plaster dried, agate stones were used to polish the surface, and a film of coconut oil was smeared over the painting. By following this rigorous process, even frescoes painted along the outsides of houses, exposed to the sun, harsh winds and the rare rain, have survived over a 100 years.

But as the Marwari families settled permanently away from their homeland, the old houses were locked up and left to decay and this art form collapsed. Art historians and art restorers working to save some of the priceless frescoes face the same problems that restorers faced at the famous Sistine Chapel in Rome. At the Vatican, Michelangelo's frescoes had been blackened by centuries of smoke from the altar candles. At Shekhawat, the large houses were left in the hands of caretakers who lit their 'chulhas' for cooking, wherever they chose to. The smoke from these chulhas have ruined many of the Shekhawati frescoes.

Censorship on the ceiling!

At the Sistine Chapel in Rome, it took Michelangelo four years to complete his frescoes. From 1508 to 1512, this artist (who was renowned more for his sculpture than his painting) lay on his back on a wooden scaffold covering every inch of the massive ceiling with scenes from the Bible. Today people from all over the world flock to see this masterpiece. But at the time Michelangelo grumbled a lot. The Pope had to first persuade, then pressurize and finally bully the reluctant sculptor to take up the assignment.

When Michelangelo completed his masterpiece and unveiled his work to his patron, Pope Paul III was shocked by what the Italians called the 'ignudi' or 'the nude'. Michelangelo had painted a number of men featured in the Biblical stories, nude! Exhausted by four years of hard labour, the artist refused to make the changes the Pope now wanted. So finally, Pope Paul got Michelangelo's student, Daniele da Volterra to paint clothes over the nude figures!

Similarly, in the fashion of those times, the Shekhawati chiteras had interspersed their frescoes of gods, automobiles and elephants with a fair sprinkling

The Emperor Who Vanished

of traditional love paintings both inside and outside the havelis. But later, the owners seemed just as scandalized by such art, as old Pope Paul III 500 years ago. And just like him, they've blacked out entire paintings.

Leonardo da Vinci's failed experiment

In 1495, da Vinci began painting 'The Last Supper' across an entire wall of a chapel in Italy. The painting is considered one of the greatest in the world, in terms of composition, the facial expressions of the people depicted and the sadness associated with the event. But as a fresco or mural, it is a failure. Da Vinci, for some reason, chose not to work on wet plaster. Like most painters comfortable working with oil paints, he liked to have the freedom to repaint, over and over again. With frescoes, that is not possible. So using the tempera technique, da Vinci painted on dry plaster, completing this project in 1498. But within a decade, the paint began to flake off, and over the centuries, constant restoration had to go on.

Chapter 7

After so many days of lunch-break-in-the-library, buried under piles of books, Nina realized that neither of them really cared about what Sir said anymore. Strangely, over this long 'punishment' they were actually having fun. Apu and she now looked through books, picked a topic they both liked and read up about it while jotting down the more interesting bits. And if they also managed to get some of what Sir wanted, great...If not, they still wrote up notes on the strange and unknown facts that they wished were in their history books.

How is it that India's sculptors who carved the most amazing works in stone remain nameless?

Travelling across India, the sheer number and beauty of the sculptures that one sees is amazing. Ancient temples will have rows of elephants running along the base, as if holding up the entire structure. There will be rows of makaras (mythical half-crocodile beasts); dancing peacocks; fierce dwarapalas standing guard at the main entrances or beautiful dwarapalikas welcoming visitors. If it is a Shiva temple, there will be a beautifully carved Nandi, the bull; maybe a shrine for Shiva's son Ganesha, and possibly a beautifully carved idol of Parvati, with a shrine of her own.

The unknown Indian artist

We are so used to seeing great sculptures all around us, that we take them for granted. We rarely wonder who the sculptor is—who were these artists who could use a chisel like a paintbrush to tell stories in stone? But India's ancient sculptors remain nameless. If there are inscriptions at temples, they record which king commissioned the building, how many surrounding villages would have to pay taxes to support the temple's upkeep—basically every single detail except the names of artistes.

We know the names of ancient Greek and Roman sculptors, thousands of years later. For instance, Lysippus, who lived in 4th century BCE, is known to us, having sculpted many of Alexander's portraits from his boyhood, on to adulthood. And everyone knows that it was Michelangelo, that famous Renaissance artist, who carved the Pieta (a marble statue of Mary with her wounded son, Jesus, on her lap).

Of the 20,000 people who slogged for years to build the Taj Mahal, only one man was allowed to sign his name—and he was the calligraphist. Across the Persian, Mughal and Arab worlds, calligraphy was considered

The Emperor Who Vanished

the highest art form, so only the master calligraphist at the Taj was allowed to sign off as 'Written by the insignificant being, Amanat Khan Shirazi.'

Rare signatures from the past

It was only when the Hoysala dynasty ruled parts of south India, from 1000 CE to the 14th century, that sculptors got their due. Across the Hoysala regions covering Hassan and other districts of Karnataka are hundreds of Vishnu, Shiva and Jain temples. And in almost all of them you can read the sculptor's proud signature engraved on stone.

One of the recurring names in Hoysala-era temples is Mullithamma. His stone 'signature' can be found in about forty Hoysala temples. Not only did Mullithamma sign his name, sculptors like him even added their guilds' names, and possibly even the names of their home towns, suddenly giving us viewers almost a 1,000 years later a brief 'glimpse' of a real Indian sculptor from centuries ago. Other names of sculptors that crop up are Bochana, Kedaroja, Keroja, Sarasvatidasu and dozens of others. And because names like Mullithamma appeared in so many temples, art historians could actually study varying styles and compare them. The work of another sculptor Baichoja or Bhaichoda appears alongside Mullithamma's at the Hoysala temple at Nuggehalli.

Isn't it strange, that only for a brief few centuries stretching from 1000 CE to 1270 CE, and only in parts of Karnataka, could talented sculptors proudly sign their names?

Other unusual features of Hoysala temples

Apart from celebrating their talented sculptors, in Hoysala temples built across south India, historians have found many other unique features. The Hoysaleshwara temple in Halebeedu, Hassan, had two garbhagrihas in the dviti vimana style, which was not very common. Usually, when a temple has two sanctum sanctora, each one features a different god. But at Halebeedu, both garbhagrihas have identical lingas in them. One seems to be the idol the king worshiped and the other was where the queen worshiped—one is called the Shantaleshwara shrine (Queen Shantala was the wife of Vishnuvardhana, the king who built this Shiva temple) and the other is called the Hoysaleshwara shrine.

The Chennakeshava temple in Belur, Hassan, was also built by the same king, and is dedicated to Lord Vishnu. Yet it also has Shaivaite, Jain and Buddhist icons across the temple complex, reflecting the religious tolerance practiced across the kingdom. The Hoysala kings also built many Jain temples.

Mughal-era Selfies!

India has a long tradition of wall painting. But like in many parts of the world, the artists remain unknown to us.

Things changed in India during the Mughal period. This dynasty loved art. The kings invited artists from Persia to India. Humayun started this tradition. Having lived in exile for a few months at the Persian court, he got to know these artists personally and he invited them to the Mughal court.

His son Akbar invested even more money in the royal karkhana or studio. Artists from all over India joined his studio and learned from each other. By Jahangir's time, signing their work became quite common among artists from the royal studio.

A well-known artist, Payag, has happily added himself to a court scene ('Jahangir presents Prince Khurram with a turban ornament'). He's unobtrusively looking away from the viewer, at the bottom left corner. His elder brother Balchand, also from the royal studio, did the same, on and off. In the case of less confident artists who didn't add themselves to important royal events or who weren't good at portraits, their names were inscribed at the back of the painting. Most artists in the Mughal studios worked to illustrate manuscripts and sometimes even added calligraphic text into their paintings to highlight the story or to praise the emperor!

This change, whereby the artist became a star in his own right, happened because of the close personal relationship the Mughal emperors developed with the artists. Jahangir conferred the title Nadir al Zaman or Zenith of the Age on his favourite artist, Abu'l Hasan. Shah Jahan preferred this artist's brother, Abid Hasan.

Chapter 8

'How many pages have we clocked up for Sir?' Nina asked, her glasses perched on the tip of her nose as she raced through the pages of some historical thriller, giving 'research' a total break.

She wasn't really listening when Apu said, 'About ten or so...we're a long way from forty.' In fact she no longer cared. In her deliciously suspenseful book, the thief of some priceless antique manuscript had given the bumbling police the slip. Since the manuscript had been stolen from the Khuda Baksh museum in Patna, she happened to mention that to Apu. This got him all excited, and into research mode. So while he filled up pages of notes, she read on. Mathur Sir was the last person on her mind.

A world renowned library in India grew out of a private collection

A family bitten by the collector bug

During the late 1800s, Khuda Baksh, a lawyer from Patna, spent long hours toiling away as a government pleader. This was his day job. He desperately needed this income to feed his passion—collecting rare books and manuscripts. It was a passion that ran in the family. When his father Maulvi Mohammed Baksh died, he gave his son his own collection of 1,800 rare manuscripts (some that he'd inherited from *his* father). He begged him to start a library that would be open to the general public. This was a very noble cause, no doubt, but the family didn't really have the money to finance such grand plans.

One of the finest collections of Islamic literature

Yet Khuda Baksh went on to build up one of the finest libraries in the East. Other than the Topkapi museum in Istanbul, the Khuda Baksh Oriental Library in Patna has the single largest collection of Islamic literature, anywhere in the world.

Khuda Baksh travelled extensively, looking for his treasures. And since he could only cover India, he hired the services of a book buyer who sourced rare manuscripts for him from the Middle East. By 1891, Khuda Baksh had built a separate library, at his own expense (of Rs 88,000 which in those days was a fortune), transferred all the books into it and threw it open to the public. By this time, the number of rare manuscripts had grown to 4,000, apart from thousands of printed books. He called this the Patna Oriental Public Library (after his death at the age of sixty-six, it was given his name).

The viceroy is impressed

This fabulous collection immediately attracted book lovers from all over the world. Lord Curzon, himself a serious scholar, deputed an Indologist named Denisson

Ross to the library to help Baksh make descriptive catalogues of the collection. He even helped set up the Lord Curzon Reading Room adjacent to the library. Other donors from all over the world contributed to this world-class collection—books arrived from Persia, the USA, Italy, Saudi Arabia and present-day Pakistan.

Four books in this library have been declared Vigyan Nidhi (or national treasures) by the National Mission for Manuscripts—two are in Persian and two in Arabic. The library is also one of the few places in the world that has a number of books from the Cordoba Library in southern Spain that got destroyed by the Catholic Spaniards, when they defeated the last Moorish kings. Among the treasures are:

- *Tarikh-I Khandha Timurah*, an illustrated manuscript commissioned by Emperor Akbar himself, on the life and family tree of Timur. This book was obviously in the royal Mughal library because two generations later, Shah Jahan wrote a personal note in it!
- The oldest handwritten copy of the *Jahangir-nama*, which once belonged to the personal collection of King George V.

- A Persian manuscript on medicinal plants and pharmacology called *Kitabi Hashaish.*
- A book called *Diwani Hafiz* by the Persian writer Hafiz Shirazi, that has personal comments written by both Humayun and his grandson Jahangir in the margins.
- Rescued from the Cordoba Library is an Islamic medical text on surgery.

A snub for the British Museum!

Khuda Baksh was conferred the title Khan Bahadur for his social service, and was also made CIE (Companion of the Order of the Indian Empire) in 1903. He served as the Chief Justice of the Hyderabad kingdom under the Nizam, for three years. But he was still short of funds. What began as a collection of 4,000 manuscripts, had grown four fold. All that book-buying left Khuda Baksh penniless when he fell ill. After he died, the Government of Bengal cleared his meagre medical bills of Rs 8,000—an amount Khuda Baksh would have happily spent on a manuscript rather than on a doctor! In fact, when the British Museum had made this bibliophile a handsome offer for his entire collection, he refused!

Kavitha Mandana

In the Deed of Trust that Baksh wrote, handing over the library to the public, his condition was that the collection would remain in Patna. In 1969, by an Act of Parliament, the Khuda Baksh Oriental Library came under the central government. And today, it's one of the few world-class libraries in the country, attracting scholars from across the globe. It also has a good collection of Sanskrit books and manuscripts, as well as a great collection of miniatures. Its manuscripts now number over 21,000 and the books add up to over 2.5 lakh titles.

Private collections

The best exhibits in other museums in India and abroad are often private collections, donated to the public. A large chunk of the collection at Mumbai's Chhatrapathi Shivaji Maharaj Vastu Sangrahalaya (formerly the Prince of Wales Museum) is made up of collections from Sir Dorabji Tata, Sir Ratan Tata, Karl and Meherbhai Khandalavala and Purushottom Mavji.

Bangalore's art museum and college, Chitrakala Parishath, was set up on land leased by the government, but with the donations of paintings from the private collection of industrialist H. K. Kejriwal and Svetoslav Roerich's donations from his own body of work, as well as his father's.

One woman's passion for a dying craft

As a young child, Veena loved braiding hair. She experimented on her family and friends. But unlike other kids, Veena never stopped playing around with people's hair! Through the 1950s and 60s, she convinced her orthodox family to let her work in the Hindi film industry. Her first film was *Rani ki Jhansi* and she went on to style hair in over 150 films for stars like Nargis, Suraiyya, Sandhya and Nutan. And right up to her seventies, she travelled the globe, demonstrating the intricate hair styles and ornaments of India that cover 3,000 years of our history.

By the time Veena Shroff passed away a few years ago, she owned one of the largest collections of antique hair ornaments in the world. In 1994, her 700-piece collection was exhibited at the India International

Centre, New Delhi, for two years running—an unheard of honour. Her path-breaking research has been part of the curriculum for students of art and history. She was the definite authority on India's hair-styling past—she could rattle off what the women in Mohenjodaro wore in their hair nearly 2,500 years ago.

Her early exposure to classical dance styles (she even studied Manipuri), with its detailed attention to traditional hair styles, sparked her interest in India's ancient hair traditions. Even though hair ornamentation and styling—Kesha Shringara—is considered one of the sixteen important personal adornments of a woman, (solah shringar) there was never sufficient historical data available to feed Veena's interest. So she went to the temples—Konark and Khajuraho, Belur and Halebid, the temples of Tamil Nadu and Andhra…these were Veena's 'textbooks'. The apsaras and dancers carved onto the brackets and panels of these centuries-old temples showed her what history books had neglected to record. And since there were no books on the subject, she wrote one after four decades of research called *Indian Hairstyles*.

Chapter 9

When Apu got worked up, his face turned red and the words tumbled out of his mouth incoherently. He spluttered, 'Did you know that at one time the Taj had been abandoned, its garden left overgrown and that British soldiers from the local garrison romanced their girlfriends among the trees on moonlit nights?' Since Nina already knew this, she looked bored. So Apu continued, 'How could the British treat one of the Wonders of the World like that?'

Nina had to get him to calm down so she said, 'Relax, you need to remember that it was the Indian rulers, the tail end of the Mughal dynasty, that had left the Taj to its fate in the first place—long before the British took control of Delhi.'

Apu looked irritated at being interrupted, but she continued, calmly, 'After Aurangzeb's long rule, the Mughal dynasty lost power across India. Over the years, local looters had stripped the Taj of the precious stones inlaid in its marble walls, its silver doors and fabulous carpets. Later the British too took what they could.'

'See…what did I tell you!' Apu burst in.

But Nina laughed and said, 'You're right…and you're also wrong, in some ways.'

'What do you mean?' Apu retorted.

'In 1830, the viceroy Lord Benedict even had a plan to demolish the monument and ship the marble to Britain, for sale. What stopped him was that there were no buyers for the marble in Britain,' Nina began.

'My point, exactly!' Apu jumped up.

'But wait,' Nina pleaded, 'Fast-forward to seventy years later, when Lord Curzon arrived in India in 1899. He had the Taj cleaned up, restored the garden and the associated structures in the Taj complex. And he got the bazaar entries to the Taj cleared…how about that?'

That calmed Apu down a bit. And as they went researching Lord Curzon, they discovered more about his Taj connections. To crown his deep appreciation for this monument, he even managed to get his name inscribed in there—not on the marble, but on an exquisite bronze lamp that he personally ordered from

Egypt, which had gold and silver inlaid work. On the lamp, in a calligraphic style that matched the other writing on the Taj's walls, is the viceroy's message of dedication to the memory of Mumtaz Mahal. For the past century, this lamp has hung above the false tombs of Mumtaz Mahal and Shah Jahan.

Strangely, the British both saved AND destroyed our ancient heritage

The missing stupa

The famous stupa at Amaravati, Andhra Pradesh, is described as one of the greatest of all the stupas built across India. The entire stupa sat on a 6-foot high circular platform surrounded by a heavily carved wall. It was founded in the 3rd century BCE. Some believe Ashoka might have started the work, but there is no conclusive proof of this. Work continued at this important Buddhist site in Guntur district, for over four centuries, upto 150 CE. And worship went on here till about the 14th century CE, after which the site was abandoned, as Buddhism died out across most of India.

But NOTHING remains of the famous Amaravati stupa currently.

In 1797, Colonel Mackenzie, a student of Indian history and a collector of antiques, discovered the Amaravati stupa in the course of his travels. Of course, he did not know it was a stupa then. But he had heard that building crews of a local zamindar, digging up a mound for construction material, had unearthed sections of carved stone. When Mackenzie went on to investigate, he sensed that he was at the site of some ancient monument. Since he had to report back to work, Mackenzie couldn't linger. He eventually came back to investigate the site only nineteen years later in 1816.

Within that time itself, the site was severely damaged, with bricks looted for construction elsewhere and broken pillars strewn about. Mackenzie soon went about unearthing what he could of the carved stone and marble friezes and shipped them out of India. Explorers and trophy hunters who came after him completed the task of flattening the stupa entirely. Mackenzie's haul now makes up the British Museum's massive collection of Buddhist-era art—the largest outside India. In fact they even have an Amaravati Gallery.

So do we need to be thankful to Mackenzie for rediscovering the stupa, or should we regret that he and the Britishers that followed sent most of it out of India?

4,000-year-old bricks to lay a railway line

In another instance of the British discovering India's ancient history, the laying of railway lines led to the discovery of many remote sites and also to their destruction, in some cases. In 1826, a man called Charles Masson noticed strange mounds across the Indus Valley. He named one of them 'the castle' and believed it needed excavation. Alexander Cunningham (the man who in 1861 became the first archaeological surveyor to the government of India and head of the Archaeological Survey of India) visited this spot twenty years later, and noted what Masson had reported, but he did nothing about it. Cunningham eventually returned in 1873, by which time, the mound and the supposed 'castle' had been flattened. The British were building the railway line between Lahore and Multan and railway contractors found the easily available bricks from the Indus Valley site very convenient, and used them to lay about 100 miles of the track.

Cunningham decided that excavations had been postponed too long, and hurriedly began work on the site, but unearthed nothing much because of the destruction already carried out. He abandoned the dig, and retired to England soon afterwards. It was only in 1920, almost 100 years after Charles Masson first alerted everyone about the 'castle', did proper work on the Indus Valley sites begin. In those 100 years of new road and rail building, a lot was destroyed.

Yet, it was the British who established the Archaeological Survey of India and the Asiatic Society. For every Mackenzie, who packed up chunks of the Amaravati Stupa and took it with him, there was a James Prinsep. His obsessive code-breaking and translation work caused him to collapse from exhaustion, but Prinsep succeeded in deciphering many of the Ashokan edicts, opening a new window to Indian history.

The Amaravati Stupa was built by many generations

of kings. This plundered stupa represents a golden age of Andhra culture. In fact, the Amaravati school of art is considered one of the three main art movements in ancient India—the others being the Gandhara school and the Mathura school. Which is why, Andhra Pradesh's new capital city will also be called Amaravati—in memory of a stupa, the dismembered parts of which are in museums across the world.

The Elliot Marbles

The British Museum is full of ancient art collected (some say plundered) from different parts of the world. Even more tragic, is that these works are named after the colonial administrators that looted them, rather than their countries or places of origin.

The 'Elliot Marbles' in the British Museum are really over 120 marble panels that Sir Walter Elliot, Collector of Guntur, shipped to London. Following in the footsteps of Mackenzie and other Britishers, Elliot is ranked amongst the most notorious of those who wrecked Amaravati.

Kavitha Mandana

The tragedy is that the British were among those who pioneered modern archaeological practices. This mandated leaving sites as they were discovered— excavating and recording for further study, but leaving the archaeological record of buildings, roads, etc, at a site undisturbed. Yet they broke their own rules as colonists.

More notorious than Elliot was the Earl of Elgin of the Elgin Marbles fame. The Elgin Marbles are really massive carved panels from the Parthenon in Athens. Elgin had agents hack them out and ship them to Britain, where he then sold them to the government. The panels were the work of the ancient Greek architect, Phidias and his team, who created them between 447 BCE and 438 BCE.

Chapter 10

It was a quiet lunch break at the library. Nina could hear the gentle snoring of the librarian on the other side of the horror books shelf. Apu, too, was nodding off over a massive book on Formula 1 cars. 'How much of history can a human take?' he had snapped when Nina had raised an eyebrow.

Suddenly, there was a flurry of activity as Mathur Sir breezed into the library, and barked, 'What Ma'am, asleep at your desk again?' at the poor librarian and stormed towards Nina and Apu.

It was too late to hide the Formula 1 glossy, or the murder mystery Nina had dipped into, 'Just to finish the chapter,' as she had promised herself.

Sir's eyes were ablaze, and his voice dripped with sarcasm, 'So if we're reading about race cars and murders on the Nile, my two super-smart star students must have finished their forty pages of research, right?'

Silence.

'RIGHT?' Sir snarled louder, as he banged the table with a clenched fist. Apu scrambled around for their notes—which were in bits and pieces all over the table and in different books. Nina sat paralyzed, like a rabbit caught in the headlights of a speeding car.

Sir snatched the differently sized sheets of paper poor Apu had managed to gather from the mess on the table. He made an elaborate act of counting the sheets, and slowly, his temper cooled down. Sighing, he put down the sheets and said, 'Twenty pages... well that's not bad...not bad at all. But it's still not forty.'

Silence.

'How much longer do you plan to take?' he asked more kindly.

Nina suddenly found her voice. 'Sir, we've run out of monuments, can we do something else?'

That was a mistake, because Sir snapped back to his earlier mood, 'Run out of monuments, she says! "Run out of" or "bored with"?'

The Emperor Who Vanished

Apu quietly said, 'Bored with, Sir. Can we do people or customs from history for the remaining pages?'

There was a long silence during which neither Apu nor Nina could read Sir's expression. Was he angry or not? Then he said, catching them off guard, 'What are all *those* notes about?'

And in response to the fake blank looks of Nina and Apu, he grinned wickedly and reached out for a thick wad of sheets held together by a large paper clip. 'This…this…let's see what else my super stars have been up to!' And with their precious notes full of 'useless information' tucked under his arm, Sir turned on his heel and walked off, adding, 'Okay, go ahead with twenty pages on people and customs, in the meantime.' And he vanished.

Nina started giggling hysterically. The whole episode was both hilarious and petrifying. And with Sir out of the way, Apu decided he had a right to make some noise too, so he banged on the table, with frustration.

'God knows how he'll react now…he's so unpredictable,' he said.

'He may even burn our delicious facts and we haven't Xeroxed them,' Nina said, glumly.

'Let's look at the bright side of things for now,' Apu said, firmly. 'We're late, but he was still impressed that we'd done twenty pages. AND he's allowed us to abandon dreary buildings and go looking for interesting dead people!'

That's exactly what Nina needed. Perking up, she said, 'I know exactly the person I want to dig up facts on.'

'Who?' Apu asked. 'Someone Sir will be happy with?'

'Technically, yes...he's a king and he ruled over Gwalior...but the rest I'm not sure.' Her voice faltered and then she said, 'But you will love him...he's a total cartoon!'

Why isn't Dulha Raja, the bridegroom prince of Gwalior, in my history textbook?

Isn't it strange how history textbooks manage to leave out the most interesting people from our past? They'll give you details about warrior kings: how many were killed in a particular battle; how many elephants charged at the enemy; and how many horsemen made up the cavalry brigade. How such-and-such kingdom stretched from the Himalayas in the north to the River Tungabhadra in the south. In Nina's mind, the kings always seemed pretty similar, even if they belonged to different dynasties. This is why when she came across Dulha Raja, or the bridegroom prince, in tiny print, lost in the footnotes of a glossy book on Gwalior, she got interested. What a comical character he turned out to be!

The strangest part is that Dulha Raja hails from Gwalior, a fort associated with valour and other such war-like qualities. And he popped up in this fort's history just when its reputation for being impregnable was at its highest.

Gwalior Fort's formidable reputation

Being a mere 200 kilometres south of Delhi (in the northern part of today's Madhya Pradesh), Gwalior attracted every invader who had set sights on southern conquests. Its strategic location made it a perfect garrison for troops heading to, or retreating from the south. In 1021, it was Mahmud of Ghazni who came knocking on Gwalior's gates with a huge army behind him. But he had no idea what a tough adversary the fort was! After four days of bombarding it, he ran out of supplies and returned to Delhi, confused. For nearly a 100 years after that, the fort was managed by a string of capable rulers, till the arrival of our hero—Dulha Raja.

The lovesick hero

He came from the Kacchapaghata noble family and his real name was Veer Singh (the brave one—ironical, yes), the prince of Narwar. Of course, his subsequent actions ensured that he was the last ruler from his family. In 1128, when it was time for our prince to get married, as was the custom, he left Gwalior for Ambar for his wedding to Princess Bargurjari, daughter of Ranmal, king of Ambar. Veer Singh obviously enjoyed married life so much that he extended his honeymoon at Ambar, staying on for a whole year!

So that the affairs in his far-off state did not interfere with his romance, he handed over the responsibility of ruling Gwalior to his nephew, Parmaldeva Pratihara. And *that* was it. The capable nephew saw a huge opportunity ahead of him. He waited a polite few months and then declared himself an independent ruler. For probably the first time in its history, Gwalior fort changed hands without any bloodshed or month-long siege.

Apart from this brief comical lapse, Gwalior fort quickly regained its reputation as an elusive, impregnable fortress. In 1196, when Mahmud Ghori's forces attacked it, Gwalior held out for a whole year, in spite of being surrounded by the enemy. When it looked like supplies within the fort had run out and the chances of holding out longer were nil, Gwalior's rulers found yet another way to thwart Ghori. They surrendered the fort to Ghori's arch-rival, Iltutmish of the Delhi Slave dynasty! But even he couldn't call it his own for long. By 1200, Iltutmish found himself fighting for eleven long months to wrest the fort back from a local raja!

All these long sieges will probably make you think of the fort as a large one with vast areas to store supplies when surrounded by an enemy army. But, incredibly, this fort is like a thin finger measuring a mere 850 metres across its widest point, and a length of 2.8 kilometres. Since it came into existence in 525 CE, Gwalior changed hands no less than twenty times. Apart from its strategic importance, this beautiful fort was also a gem that every ruler somehow wanted to own. In 1527, Babur, fleeing the tiny Central Asian kingdom that he'd lost to scheming cousins, found a lot to criticize in India, but fell in love with this fort.

Legend has it that the fort was built by a local Rajput chieftain, Suraj Sen. He suffered from leprosy and one day while out hunting near a spring, asked a wandering sage for a vessel to fill drinking water with. The sage himself filled a cup of water for the nobleman, after which his leprosy disappeared! In gratitude, Suraj Sen built a tank around the spring and named it Gwalior, in honour of the sadhu, Gwalipa.

Gwalior's most famous son

Lovers of Hindustani classical music know Gwalior as the birthplace of the Gwalior gharana. India's best-known musician, Tanna Mishra, made his name here in the court of Raja Vikramjit, who renamed the ustad Tansen (or master of the musical note). Tansen subsequently moved on to become the most celebrated Navaratna of Akbar's court. When he died, the emperor himself, along with every renowned musician of the period, accompanied the funeral procession to Gwalior. And every December, in remembrance of its illustrious citizen, the fortress town holds one of north India's most famous music festivals.

During the Mughal period, the fort's 35-feet-high impregnable walls perched on clifftops 100 feet above the town and the plains below, made it an ideal spot to stash away VIP prisoners. Jahangir held Guru Hargobind Singh, the sixth Sikh guru, captive in this fort. He also exiled his eldest son Khusrau to Gwalior. Aurangzeb locked up one of his brothers, Murad, and his son, Mohamed Sultan and assorted nephews here, till their death.

During the British Raj, Rani Lakshmibai of Jhansi died here, fighting English forces during the First War of Independence. Certainly, Gwalior has had a fair share of heroes and heroines, but if Nina and Apu had to pick their favourite, it would still be the comical, lovestruck Dulha Raja.

Chapter 11

Apu was bouncing around in the library, waiting for Nina and getting irritated with each minute of delay. He knew she would be excited about the next person he'd unearthed, and that's why he couldn't wait for her to arrive. When she did, he quickly switched to acting all bored and relaxed.

'Any ideas on who else we could dig up from the graves of history today?' he asked, getting a fairly accurate imitation of Mathur Sir's sarcastic voice.

'Noooooo, in fact now I feel structures are better than people…there are so many more of them to research,' Nina grumbled.

That's when Apu revealed his trump card. 'I wondered if this might interest you,' he said, pushing across a few scribbled lines on Buddha's mother.

He was suitably rewarded for his patience as Nina's face lit up and she exclaimed, 'Wow! She sounds cool!'

Then her shoulders slumped as she glared at him. 'This is just whom I wish I'd discovered first.'

They got to work.

was the first fight for women's rights led by Buddha's foster mother?

When we think of Buddhist women, the name that first pops up in our heads is Sanghamitra, Emperor Ashoka's daughter. She, along with her brother Mahinda, travelled to Sri Lanka to preach about Buddhism and that's how the religion began its travels outside India. But Sanghamitra was following in another royal woman's footsteps.

Siddhartha, the son of Suddhodhana, a Sakya leader in what is today a region spanning northern Bihar and

Nepal, lost his mother Mayadevi when he was just a week old. He was nursed and brought up by his mother's sister Mahaprajapati, along with her own children.

We all know the details of the young Buddha's life. How astrologers told his father that this child would either be a great king or a great religious teacher. Years later, Siddhartha, then married and a father, left the palace alone in search of the truth. After he attained Nirvana, his father kept sending delegations from the palace, begging his son to return. In all, ten delegations were sent and leaders of all but the last didn't pass on the father's message but instead joined Buddha as his disciples. Eventually, Buddha returned to his father's palace, where many of his cousins, his stepbrother Nanda, his young son Rahul and his dear foster mother Mahaprajapati became Buddhists.

A non-violent fight for equal rights

When Buddha's father Suddhodhana died, his mother wanted to renounce her life in the palace and join the Buddhist order. Till then, only men had become monks. The Buddha refused to let his mother renounce her royal life and left for Rajagriha. But Mahaprajapati wasn't going to be put off—she cut off her hair, gave up her royal wardrobe, donned simple robes and followed Buddha, along with a number of other royal women. Finally, Buddha's cousin and close confidant Ananda interceded on behalf of the women, convincing Buddha that since he believed women could attain moksha, surely they could also become nuns. That's how women joined the Buddhist sangha, and were referred to as bhikhunis or theris.

This is probably the first record of women asking for and getting the same rights as men. This was centuries before Christ. After Christianity spread, a number of Catholic monastic orders for men and women emerged, starting from the 3rd century CE. But during the Buddha's lifetime around the 5th century BCE, the theris were not only the first women to demand equal rights (about 2,200 years before women in the West began fighting for their right to vote in the 1800s), but probably also the first women to renounce their lives and join a structured monastic order.

The tradition of theris and bhikhunis died out with time. In India, Buddhism went into complete decline. Today, less than 1 per cent of Indians call themselves

Buddhist. But even in countries with a majority of its population remaining Buddhist, the women's order vanished. By the 11th century CE, there were no theris in Sri Lanka. In Burma, the tradition died out in the 13th century. The practice is now being tentatively revived in the West, where Buddhism has gained in popularity, with even the Dalai Lama offering his support.

A literary first too!

Buddha taught people to give up mindless rituals and to stop blindly following the instructions of priests. He believed each person had to find their own individual path to the truth. And once they attained enlightenment, the Buddhist tradition was for people to share their personal journey. So monks and nuns wrote down, in verse, their path to enlightenment.

These songs, composed in Pali, were shared with the public while preaching about Buddhism, and passed on from older monks and nuns to younger ones, orally.

The 500-odd songs sung by the nuns are called the Therigatha, or Songs of the Elder Nuns. Some were composed during Buddha's lifetime, and others, over the subsequent period of 300 years. These were complied in an anthology in 80 BCE. And this is the first known anthology of women's writing anywhere in the world! Here is a poem by Mahaprajapati, Buddha's beloved foster mom and the first Buddhist nun. In the Buddhist tradition, it is believed that through deep meditation people are able to see and understand their past lives. So the third verse in this poem talks about that. The last verse is the author remembering her sister (Buddha's real mother), who died after giving birth to Buddha.

Buddha! Hero! Praise be to you!
You foremost among all beings!
You who have released me from pain,
And so many other beings too.

All suffering has been understood.
The source of craving has withered.
Cessation has been touched by me
On the noble eight-fold path.

I've been mother and son before;
And father, brother—grandmother too.

The Emperor Who Vanished

Not understanding what was real,
I flowed-on without finding [peace].

But now I've seen the Blessed One!
This is my last compounded form.
The on-flowing of birth has expired.
There's no more re-becoming now.

See the gathering of followers:
Putting forth effort, self controlled,
Always with strong resolution
—This is how to honour the Buddha!

Surely for the good of so many
Did Maya give birth to Gotama,
Who bursts asunder the mass of pain
Of those stricken by sickness and death.

'MahaPajapati (Gotami) Theri: A Mother's Blessing' (Thig 6.6),

translated from the Pali by Andrew Olendzki.

Chapter 12

Once they started reading about Buddhism and its spread in India and the world, Nina and Apu naturally started researching Ashoka, the emperor who embraced the religion. He was another gold mine of data with enough details of the length and breadth of the Mauryan empire to keep Sir happy, and a whole bunch of other strange details to keep their own curiosity aroused.

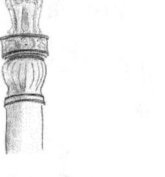

How very strange that Emperor Ashoka vanished from history for about 2,000 years!

If dead emperors toss in their graves, then Ashoka must

certainly have done so...for about 2,000 years! No ruler in India has conquered so much territory—not the great Mughals who came about 1,600 years after Ashoka, nor the British who ruled large parts of India for about 200 years. Yet, barely fifty years after Ashoka died in 232 BCE, the Mauryan dynasty came to an end and everyone forgot about him. This happened in spite of him leaving detailed messages to the people of his empire, engraved on rock faces and on tall stately stone pillars that have survived for 2,200 years.

Right from the time he won the brutal battle of Kalinga in 262-61 BCE, Ashoka had been filled with remorse. At a time in history when kings were judged by the battles they won and their performance on the battlefield, Ashoka announced he was giving up war. He turned away from the horrors of the battlefield and embraced Buddhism.

50-metre-tall, 5-tonne government circulars

Ashoka had his message of peace, non-violence and the deep regret he felt about his own violent past inscribed all over his empire. These famous edicts can still be read on rock faces and pillars across India. Ashoka's empire was the biggest India would ever see. It stretched from Kandahar in Afghanistan, across Peshawar in the Northwest in Pakistan, right across India to Bangladesh. And from Kashmir right down to Kurnool in Andhra Pradesh. To make sure everyone understood his message of peace, the inscriptions were in different languages. Across most parts of present-day India, it was in Brahmi, which was the common script of those days. In the Northwest, close to Peshawar, Ashoka's message was inscribed in Kharoshti, which is derived from the Aramaic script used in Persia. Another edict found close to Kandahar in Afghanistan has the message etched in stone in two languages—Aramaic and Greek!

His edicts were written for not just the citizens of his empire, but even for their descendants. He wanted his message of non-violence and tolerance to be remembered by generations after him. But sadly, that was not to be. Ashoka died in 232 BCE. And barely fifty years later, in 180 BCE, the Mauryans were gone. Their vast empire disintegrated quickly under a succession of weak rulers.

A tolerant, secular dynasty

Ashoka's grandfather and founder of the Mauryan dynasty was a Jain; his father Bindusara was also not a Hindu but an Ajivika (a sect that did not believe in Karma); and he himself was a Buddhist. Subsequent kings in India were predominantly Hindu and probably saw no reason to keep alive the memory of this 'non-conformist' dynasty! Buddhism died out across India, though it spread abroad in Sri Lanka, South East Asia, China and Japan. Ashoka's son Mahenda preached Buddhism in Sri Lanka, where the royal family adopted Buddhism. If Buddhism had survived in India, maybe Ashoka's name would have been kept alive.

Code name 'Piyadasi'

There could be other reasons for Ashoka's 2,000-year exile from history books. One was that Ashoka never referred to himself by his own name nor used the Mauryan name in his inscriptions. Each edict began as a message from 'Devanamapiya' (the Beloved of the Gods') and 'Piyadasi' (one who looks with kindness upon everything). Subsequent generations had no idea who this Beloved of the Gods was. The edicts were also mostly written in Brahmi, the ancient language that was used in Ashoka's time. But when the language and knowledge of the script died out, people couldn't read what was written on those edicts. The multilingual Greek and Aramaic edict could have played a role in keeping Ashoka in the public memory because during Mauryan times, the western-most areas of the empire had a Greek population, left over after Alexander's conquests a few decades before Ashoka's time.

But the Greeks either migrated back or intermarried locally, so very soon after Ashoka's death, in the regions near Kandahar, Greek was no longer in use. Ashoka had to wait centuries until 1837 before India rediscovered him.

Prinsep, a self-taught linguist

James Prinsep was an English amateur Indologist who worked at the Bengal Mint. He had taught himself quite a few of India's dead languages, as he became interested in old coins. With his talent for 'code breaking', he was able to translate one of Ashoka's edicts from Brahmi into English. For those interested in Indian history, this was a major breakthrough.

The Emperor Who Vanished

Yet it was frustrating to have this mystery king's edict translated and still not know who he was. As Prinsep struggled over this problem, in Sri Lanka, another British civil servant translated a Buddhist Pali manuscript call *Mahavamsa*. This was a collection of histories of Ceylon, written by Buddhist monks. In this book, Ashoka is not just mentioned, but revered and praised. With the inputs from Sri Lanka, Prinsep was able to deduce that the Devanamapiya of the Brahmi edicts was really Ashoka, one of India's greatest rulers.

Speaking to us across 2,000 years

Ashoka's edicts were phrased informally, and the words ring true across the centuries.

Check this little excerpt:

The Beloved of the Gods does not consider gifts of honour to be as important as the essential advancement of all sects. Its basis is the control of one's speech, so as not to extol one's own sect or disparage that of another, on unsuitable occasions...

The 'original' Rosetta Stone?

In 1799, French soldiers in Egypt looking to conquer the country before the English could, stumbled on a stone plaque in a town called Rosetta (the locals called it Rashid). Experts stated that the stone had been engraved in 196 BCE. It was written in three languages—Greek (the language of the last Ptolemy Pharaohs, who were descendants of Alexander's governor); in Egyptian hieroglyphics; and in Demotic, the language of the common people. Since Greek was well known to the 18th-century scholars, the Greek translation was the basis on which the other two languages could be decoded. It took French experts twenty-three years to crack the hieroglyphics.

Ashoka's bilingual edict at Kandahar predates the Rosetta stone by about fifty years. If only some scholars had discovered it earlier, the Greek part of the edict could have been the key to deciphering the Aramaic part. Then the world would have known about Ashoka, his great empire and reforming zeal, centuries earlier.

The Emperor Who Vanished

Chapter 13

Nina was reading up on the collapse of the Mughal empire and had begun following Nadir Shah through the pages of history books. She was interested in what had happened to the famous Peacock Throne. Nina had hoped that she would figure out if and when the throne was dismantled and its precious stones sold, or whether some other king had stolen it from Nadir Shah. But she never got to the bottom of that mystery, because she got distracted by a bunch of elephants!

Why elephants and camels paraded through St Petersburg one freezing winter!

Imagine not just fourteen elephants draped in luxurious

fabric from India, but also a street-long caravan of camels and mules laden with treasures from India parading down the freezing streets of St Petersburg, Russia. All that was on show was stolen goods...even the elephants; or what is called 'war booty'.

Nadir Shah goes looking for loot

In 1739, two of the most powerful empires in the East were in decline. After Aurangzeb's death, the Mughals were no longer powerful emperors, their territory having shrunk considerably. And in Iran, the empire of the Safavids, who had ruled since 1502, was also disintegrating. It was this massive power vacuum that Nadir Shah stepped into. He was a poor Persian boy from a nomadic tribe close to the Afghan border. He managed to escape abject poverty, and joined forces with those trying to evict the Afghans from Persia. As his group won small battles, he rose up through the ranks to become their leader.

When Persia lost territory to its neighbours—to the Ottoman Turks on the west and to the Russians to the north—Nadir Shah stepped up to help the Shah drive out the invaders. Soon, he won the people's support because he successfully chased the Afghans out of Iran and fought the Ottoman Turks to recapture lost Persian territories. And because he'd achieved all this in such a short time, he was able to convince the Russians to return areas that they had annexed because of the weak Safavid Shah...even without a battle. With such victories under his belt, Nadir Shah deposed the Safavid Shah and declared himself the country's leader. But winning so many wars within such a short span of time had emptied Persia's treasuries, so Nadir Shah looked eastwards for funds.

The Mughal empire was crumbling just three generations after Aurangzeb had died an old man. The Mughal on the throne, Mohammed Shah, was 'emperor' only in name. When Nadir Shah attacked India, the Mughals lost the crucial battle at Karnal. This gave Nadir Shah the keys to the Mughal treasury, which had been built up over 200 years. Apart from the Kohinoor diamond and the famous Peacock Throne, a lot of the treasures Nadir Shah's army took back on thousands of elephants was looted from the Delhi nobility—over days of street fighting, brutal killings and chaos.

As his long caravan of war booty returned, prior to crossing the Indus river, Nadir Shah sent off two embassies, one to Russia and one to Ottoman Turkey. Both included elephants and camels laden with treasures looted from Delhi. It almost seemed like showing off (or like a veiled threat), saying to his competitors, 'Look what I got…it's enough to finance any war I choose to fight!' The wealth Nadir Shah took back was so immense that he waived taxes in his country for three straight years.

The elephant caravan

The camels and elephants destined for Russia left the banks of the Indus in the first half of 1739. The convoy, led by the ambassador, included 16,000 people! But such a vast number made slow progress. It had to cross the Hindu Kush mountains and travel over 6,000 kilometres. It was only in October 1740 that this moving 'embassy' reached St Petersburg. But they had trouble on the way. When the 16,000-strong caravan arrived in the southern Russian city of Astrakhan, the authorities panicked. This looked suspiciously like an army to them, not a gift-laden embassy. So they only allowed 4,000 people to accompany the gifts and the elephants.

In Russia, meanwhile, the purpose of this gift-laden caravan was viewed in an entirely different light. The royal family believed that Nadir Shah hoped to marry the Tsarseva (or princess) Elizabeth, daughter of Peter the Great. She was known to be a great beauty, and such an alliance would also make Russia and Persia allies. But Elizabeth did not seem interested in being one among Nadir Shah's vast harem.

A fine art preserved in a far-off land

This is why some of the most exquisite Indian metalwork anywhere in the world is only found in the Hermitage Museum in St Petersburg, the winter capital of Russia in those days and at the Topkapi museum in Istanbul, Turkey. Even the British were able to collect very few Mughal-era gold, silver and bronze work because, in India, the moment anything got even slightly damaged, the ornament or vessel would be melted and reworked into something else. So very few samples of goblets, hookahs, paan platters and precious jewellery survive from the Mughal era...and of course, what hadn't been melted down, got carted off by invaders like Nadir Shah.

It made Nina wonder how the fourteen elephants coped with the Russian winter. After being unloaded were they sent off to warmer climates, like down south to Astrakhan where the River Volga joins the Caspian Sea? Were the Russians able to breed them in captivity, like in India?

Lost and found

For years, the gold treasures that accompanied the elephants were stored at the Hermitage, a museum in St Petersburg that showcases the Russian Tsars' collections over generations. Later, when 20th-century curators were looking over the vast collections of the Hermitage, they assumed that the beautiful pieces were Persian, since they were probably entered in some ledger back in 1740 as gifts from Nadir Shah. The ledger records twenty-two beautiful objects and fifteen rings of gold and precious stones but only seventeen gem-encrusted gold and silver objects and only one of the rings survive. Inscribed on this ring was the name: The Second Sahibkiran. To any expert of Islamic history and art, this instantly flagged the collection as Indian. Why? Because that was one of the official names of Shah Jahan! Sahibkiran described a person born during extremely auspicious circumstances, in terms of planetary alignments.

Elephants in the Snow

In 218 BCE, Hannibal was a brilliant general of the Carthage empire that stretched all along North Africa on the Mediterranean coast. Rome and Carthage were at war. Hannibal had decided to take the fight to Roman territory, so he crossed the sea and landed his army of 100,000 soldiers and thirty-seven elephants in Spain. There he fought the Romans and the Gauls. The battle didn't end there.

In an unimaginable feat, Hannibal then marched his soldiers, horsemen and elephants towards Italy, crossing the Alps and attacked Rome from the north. The Romans were stunned, and being caught unprepared, lost a series of battles to Hannibal as he charged further and further south, closer to Rome. Hundreds of thousands of Romans died in these battles, demoralized and terrorized by elephants, an animal they'd never seen before.

Hannibal eventually returned to Carthage, but without capturing Rome. Sadly, apart from the thousands of soldiers he lost in this war, he returned with only one elephant...the one he rode and whom he called Surrus, which implied 'the Syrian'.

Syria never had native elephants, but during that period, in an exchange of gifts with an Indian king, Syrian rulers received a number of elephants sent along with Indian ambassadors. Later, in a battle with Egypt, the Egyptians captured these elephants and brought them back to North Africa. Since the Egyptians and Cartheginians were allies, some Indian elephants are believed to have come to Carthage.

This seems plausible, because of two reasons. One, North Africa, too, did not have an elephant population. Elephants roamed the African plains only from below the Sahara. Also, African elephants have never been domesticated or trained like Asian elephants. So strange though it seems, over 2,200 years ago, a 'regiment' of elephants faced a far more arduous trek than the fourteen elephants sent to Russia in 1739 CE.

Chapter 14

Nina's mom had packed her famous chicken biriyani in the lunch box, and even though she'd shared some with her friends, she still felt stuffed. So within minutes of arriving at the library, she laid her head on the table and dozed off. She was going to be alone today, because Apu, having managed to break a flat-bottomed flask in the lab, was now being lectured to by the principal.

Just as she was floating off into a pleasant half nap, she was woken up by a tap on her shoulder. Nina's first thought was Mathur Sir, but thankfully, it was the librarian. And she didn't look angry or like she was going to launch into a lecture on 'The Evils of Sleeping in the Library'. Instead she handed over a tattered encyclopaedia to Nina, with a bright pink Post-it sticking out of one page.

'You might find this man Rheede interesting, for

your terribly punishing project,' she said with a smile, as she walked away.

She was right. Rheede had Nina hooked, but the man who followed in Rheede's footsteps 300 years later, even more so.

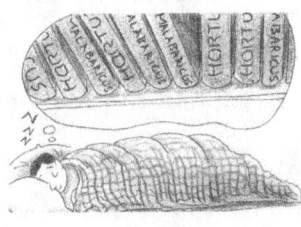

A Botany book that became the life's work of two men, 300 years apart

Before the English arrived, the Dutch were in India

Commodore Henrik von Rheede arrived in Kerala in the late 17th century. He was to look after the Dutch East India Company's interests in the Malabar region. It was a time when the Dutch, the Portuguese, the English and the French all had trading centres in India.

As governor of Dutch Malabar, and as a senior administrator of the company, Rheede had travelled across Sri Lanka, India's Coromandel (east) coast and Java, where the Dutch had set up either colonies or trading centres. He was particularly impressed by what he saw in the Malabar region. The rich local biodiversity and the region's centuries-old trade in spices and herbs made him realize that this area was a gold mine of trading opportunities.

As governor, he set up a team of over twenty-five people to collect, name and describe the medicinal properties of all local plants. The team was truly multiracial as it was made up of Dutch and Portuguese priests, illustrators, botanists, plant gatherers and locals with knowledge of Ayurveda. Remarkably, Rheede gave the Indian experts the leading roles. The 'Malabar region' that they studied was defined by Rheede as the forests and coastline along the Western Ghats, from Goa down to Kanyakumari. The Indian team members were three Konkani-speaking Goud Saraswat brahmins—Ranga Bhat, Vinayak Bhat and Appu Bhat—whose knowledge of local fauna and their medicinal properties had been passed on to them as an oral tradition, over generations. But the lead role was assigned to a practicing vaidyan or doctor from the Ezhava community, Karapuram Itty Achudhan.

Led by Achudhan, teams of men collected around 740 medicinal plants. These were illustrated with great care and after much debate and consensus between the Indian team members, the names of each plant was recorded in four languages—Malayalam, Nagari/Sanskrit, Arabic and Latin. Achudhan also spoke some Portuguese, so while he wrote in Malayalam about the medicinal plants and how they ought to be used, he could also converse with Emmanuel Carneiro, a resident of Cochin who translated his work into Portuguese. This record was then translated into Latin, the common language of science across Europe.

The Garden of Malabar

After years of careful, systematic work, Rheede began publishing the book, *Hortus Malabaricus* or *Garden of Malabar* (in twelve volumes of about 500 pages each) in Amsterdam. The first volume came out in 1678. And by 1693, the twelfth and last volume was in print.

Rheede lived to see most of his hard work in print, but he died in 1691, missing the last couple of volumes.

The books caused a sensation in Europe. They were even acknowledged by Carl Linnaeus, about fifty years later, as a superb research resource prior to publishing his own famous books on plant taxonomy, *Systema Naturae* and *Species Plantarum*. But soon, the twelve-volume Latin series became outdated. Since it came out in the pre-Linnaean period, later botanists found it difficult to identify or study the plants mentioned. And across Europe, Latin had stopped being the language used for science.

The *Hortus Malabaricus* is an important social, historical and botanical work. It is the oldest book on Indian plant collections. It is the first time Malayalam words appeared in print, *anywhere*. The Indian language words were engraved in copper, like the illustrations, because in 1678, when *Hortus* was published, there was no movable type for Indian scripts. The book also tells us how much Malayalam has changed over 300 years.

Apart from that, the book is the result of close cooperation between many people that we tend to think of as adversaries. The Dutch had fought and evicted the Portuguese from Cochin and Cannanore, yet there were Portuguese on the *Hortus* team. The Dutch had also fought against the King of Cochin, and later their relations with the Zamorin of Calicut soured. Yet, Rheede had both rulers' support for his massive project. And typically, Brahmins and Ezhavas never worked together, yet the three Brahmins signed on to the project first, stayed on and collaborated, even when Itty Achudhan came on, somewhat in the lead role.

Manilal's obsession

About 300 years later, a young boy in Kozhikode became interested in the books. Kattungal Subramaniam, Manilal's father, read widely, and often talked about the *Hortus Malabaricus*. Later, Manilal studied botany in Calicut University and did his Masters at Sagar in Madhya Pradesh. In 1969, during a college visit to the Forest Research Institute (earlier the Imperial Forest College), he saw the twelve Latin volumes of *Hortus Malabaricus* in the institute's library and it fired his imagination. Manilal is reported to have said that knowing no Latin, he still spent time copying out the Malayalam names for the plants featured.

If Rheede's work could be called a grand obsession, there can be no words for Manilal's passion. Over the next forty years, this professor from Calicut University decided to translate the twelve volumes of *Hortus Malabaricus* into English, and make the book widely accessible. He taught himself Latin first. He travelled to Cochin once a month for two- or three-day-long classes with an old priest, Father Anthony Mukkuth. And when the old man died, Manilal plodded on. He took about two to three years to translate each 500-page Latin volume.

A true-blue botanist

Manilal's ambitions went beyond mere translation. He was a world-renowned botanist, having had his papers published in leading science journals across the world. So he and his team went searching for each and every specimen that Itty Achudhan had collected 300 years ago, checked their names and descriptions and re-classified them according to the current Linnaean system. He told a newspaper that of the 750+ plants, only one called *chentani* couldn't be found.

This long journey of translation and re-identification was driven primarily by Manilal's passion, some limited personal funds and two grants—one from the UGC (1975-78) and one from the Smithsonian Institute (1984-87).

The twelve volumes translated by Manilal were published by the University of Kerala in 2003. And by 2008, Manilal with the help of language experts, had got all the volumes translated back to Malayalam, the language in which Itty Achudhan had first recorded his contributions! According to Manilal, under the Linnaean-derived ICBN (International Code of Botanical Nomenclature), of the plant names derived from Indian languages, the most are from Malayalam, all thanks to Itty Achudhan, whose knowledge so impressed a Dutch governor 325 years ago, that he worked with him as an equal.

Chapter 15

If there was one thing that interested Nina and Apu more than long dead historical people and places, it was accounts of ghosts, ghouls and spirits. Imagine their delight when they found this story of Captain Robert Gill in a tattered copy of an Asiatic Society journal.

Could there be any truth to the strange curse of the Ajanta Caves?

No tigers, but lots of art!

In 1819, British soldiers from the Madras Regiment,

out on manoeuvres in the Sahaydri Hills, decided to go tiger hunting. Instead, they stumbled upon the ancient Buddhist cave temples at Ajanta. The 1,500-year-old wall murals depicted scenes from the life of the Buddha and the Bodhisattvas. The many centuries in between had dimmed but not destroyed the vibrancy of colours and the delicacy of the lines.

About twenty-five years later, when James Ferguson, an avid Indophile visited the caves, he was disturbed by their condition. Now that people knew about them, the caves were being vandalised. He complained to the East India Company that if copies of the ancient murals were not made quickly, they'd be lost forever.

At that time, the area around Ajanta near Aurangabad was dense jungle, where the fierce Bhil tribe lived. According to the local legend about Ajanta, Lord Indra had given all the gods a day off to enjoy on earth, and they had to get back to heaven before dawn. But the gods were having such a good time down here, they forgot their curfew timing and overstayed. So in anger, Indra froze them into paintings on the walls of the Ajanta caves! The locals believed that copying those paintings would be defiling or dishonouring the gods, thus inviting their anger.

A cushy life copying Ajanta art

In response to Ferguson's alarmed and urgent call, the East India Company sent Captain Robert Gill, a soldier who was also known to paint, to do the job. Gill was a member of the Asiatic Society and was profoundly impressed by the Ajanta murals. Happy to be relieved of his army responsibilities, he got to work immediately. The curse of Ajanta didn't affect him personally. He lived on till a ripe seventy five, at a time when life expectancy of the English in India wasn't very high. He got paid Rs 200 (quite a lot in those days) over and above his salary to do what he loved. And having sent off his wife and children to England, he married a beautiful Indian woman called Paroo—all of which sounds more like a boon from Lord Indra, than a curse.

The curse at work?

But Gill's *paintings* were jinxed—they seem to have faced Indra's wrath. For the next twenty years he worked at Ajanta, living mostly in the caves, even though a neglected palace was offered to him. He kept shipping off batches of life-sized painted copies of Ajanta's art to England via Bombay. But tragedy first struck in 1866. His paintings were on display at the Crystal Palace in London, when fire broke out. Sadly, all but four or five of his paintings got burnt. Worse still, no one had made painted copies of Gill's work, nor taken photographs of them. Besides, over the twenty-year period of his work, some of the murals that Gill had painted had gotten even more damaged beyond repair or recognition. Heartbroken, a tired Gill decided to start over again. But by this time he had also taken up photography. Today, many of his prints survive, but barely four of his paintings.

In the 1870s, a batch of art students from Bombay took on the task of redoing what Gill had done. And when those paintings were sent off and displayed at the Victoria and Albert Museum…fire broke out there too! Along with this next lot, one more of Gill's originals got burnt.

Eventually, after decades of work, only four paintings of Gill's survived and now hang in the V&A.

The curse of the Pharaohs

In the days of the pharaohs in ancient Egypt, a royal burial involved priceless artefacts being buried along with the dead ruler. So being a grave robber was a profitable career. While Egyptian architects designed tombs to confuse thieves with false doors and tunnels that led nowhere, grave robbers still wormed their way through tonnes of stone boulders into the tombs. Instilling terror about the 'power of curses' was the only option left to royal families who didn't want their dear departed to be disturbed by grave robbers. But even this wasn't too effective.

In 1891, a young treasure seeker called Howard Carter landed in Egypt. He was certain there had to be some royal graves still intact. In 1907, he got financial backing from the rich Lord Carnarvon. But year after year, Carter got nowhere closer to ancient treasure. After about fifteen years, Lord Carnarvon lost patience and told Carter that there would be no more funding. But somehow Carter, himself no longer a young man, bargained for just one more year of financial support. And luckily for him, that's when he discovered King Tutankhamen's tomb…untouched by tomb raiders!

Kavitha Mandana

It was during Lord Carnarvon's second trip to Egypt in 1923, after King Tut's tomb had been found, that he fell ill and died. He was fifty-seven, and an infected mosquito bite led to septicaemia, then pneumonia and eventual death at the Savoy in Cairo. But it could hardly have been the Pharaoh's curse. Carnarvon was one of the early auto-enthusiasts. Being rich and reckless, he was known to drive around at high speed on roads that weren't too good in those days (in cars that had none of the safety measures of today). In 1901, twenty-two years before King Tut's tomb was touched, Carnarvon had a near-fatal accident, from which he never made a complete recovery.

For years, though, the press tried to sensationalize the 'Mummy's Curse' but Carter himself lived on to his sixties. And so did most others associated with the dig.

Chapter 16

'I'm beginning to worry about Mathur Sir,' Apu said, one afternoon. They'd managed about fourteen pages on 'People from History', most of them a boring line-up of kings, queens and ministers.

'So long as he leaves us alone, I'm happy,' Nina said, adding, 'I'd rather we finished before he swoops in here again.'

They'd taken to hiding their 'own' notes, in case of a surprise visit.

'I'm worried about what he's done with our notes on ancient monuments. He's quite capable of shredding them, calling them "totally useless".'

But they both soon forgot Sir, because they were on the trail of an interesting Frenchman.

Strange that a French astronomer found what archaeologists missed on the eastern coast of India

Chasing Venus

In 1760, Pondicherry was a French port. At that time, astronomers across the world had begun to get excited about the planet Venus crossing between the Earth and the sun, an event calculated to occur on 1 June 1761. Many European countries sent off scientific missions across the globe. Astronomer Edmund Halley had suggested that precisely recording the event from different corners of the world, as it occurred, would help calculate the distance between the Earth and the sun. So a French aristocrat and astronomer called Jean Baptiste Gentil de la Galaisiere (that is just the second half of his name!) set off from France.

He reached Mauritius, then a French port, and stayed awhile, but his journey onwards was a disaster. His ship lost its way in a storm in the Indian Ocean, and as June 1 approached, his captain discovered that Pondicherry had been invaded by the British. So when Venus crossed the sun, this poor astronomer was on board a rocking ship and his readings were of no use.

Most such planetary occurrences are paired events, so the next crossing of Venus was due in 1769. An optimistic Jean Baptiste Gentil decided to remain in the East for those years, studying local geography, weather, etc., anything that would help studies in the French Academy of Science. He decided to head to the Philippines, but there the Spanish mistook him for a spy. He avoided getting imprisoned by discovering that the French had wrested Pondicherry back from the English, so he managed to escape from Manila by ship.

An eleven-year Pondicherry holiday

He spent the next few years happily in Pondicherry, much feted by the local French governor, but all his preparations to take readings of Venus' next crossing, failed again, as it turned cloudy on the crucial date! Dejected, this astronomer fell ill. And while recuperating before his long journey back to France discovered an ancient settlement on the banks of River Ariyankuppam!

This place was called Arikamedu. Though his expertise was in astronomy, Jean Baptiste Gentil was certain this was an ancient city waiting to be excavated. But he had to rush back home. He'd been away eleven years, and his family, certain that he was dead, had begun dividing his property back in France!

Excavations begin

Two hundred years later this astronomer's hunch was proved right by archaeologists. A Frenchman, Jouveau Dubreuil excavated the site in 1940. And what he found suggested that Arikamedu had been trading with Imperial Rome in ancient times. What Dubreuil found was collected and stashed away, to be studied and analyzed later because World War II had broken out.

In 1944, Sir Mortimer Wheeler, the renowned archaeologist was the head of the ASI. The war was raging across the globe. While the whole of Europe had been turned into a multi-front battlefield, in the East, the British Empire was fighting the Japanese. Losing Singapore to the Japanese had been a humiliating blow for the English. From then on, the Japanese had swiftly overrun Thailand and defeated the English in innumerable battles in the jungles of Burma.

How the Japanese led the English to the Romans!

Japanese bombers had targeted Calcutta and since 1942, the city had faced black-outs. Vijayawada had been bombed, and the port blockaded by Japanese ships and submarines in the Bay of Bengal. The next target was expected to be Madras. After the fall of Burma, refugees had flooded Madras, and shared horror stories of how the English had evacuated Rangoon—the British travelling first class, and the Indians left to walk hundreds of miles under fire from the Japanese army. Not expecting the English to protect Indians, that April in 1944, a third of Madras' Indian population left the city, most of them on foot and bullock cart. While the British travelled first class by train to the Nilgiris!

In this abandoned city, Mortimer Wheeler paced restlessly through the Madras museum, waiting for the

Japanese bombs to fall. They never did. The Japanese ships were called back to take on a revived US fleet in the Pacific.

While he was at the museum, in a dusty cupboard in one corner, Wheeler discovered an ancient amphora, the two-handled jar that was used across the Mediterranean coast to store wine. He found out that this had been excavated at Arikamedu, close to Pondicherry. Wheeler knew he'd stumbled onto something important. In Pondicherry, he found collections of pottery shards that he instantly recognized as Arrentine ware, known to all scholars of the Roman Empire as being made in the town of Arezzo. This meant that Romans had been trading with Arikamedu 2,000 years ago!

From Takshila to Arikamedu

This was a sensational discovery, but Wheeler had to be patient. The war was going on and the ASI had limited funds and staff. The next summer, Wheeler felt Arikamedu was important enough to shift his team from Takshila. There was a sense of urgency for many reasons. Being so close to Pondicherry, Wheeler knew the French too would get back to excavating after the war…and there was a healthy competition between scholars from both countries.

After twelve days of digging, Wheeler's team found enough evidence to establish that Arikamedu had been trading with Imperial Rome.

A lot to excavate

Later excavations at Arikamedu occurred between 1947 and 1950, conducted by a French team led by Jean Marie Casal. And even later, by archaeologist Vimala Begley, between 1989 and 1992, heading a joint team from the Madras Museum and the University of Pennsylvania.

Vimala Begley's three-year study showed that Arikamedu had been trading with Rome from about 200 BCE to about 200 CE. But long after the Roman Empire collapsed, this busy port continued to thrive under the Pallavas, Cholas and Pandyas.

Historians have concluded that during Roman times Arikamedu was one of the leading bead manufacturing centres of the world. It also was a textile dyeing centre, and operated pretty much like today's SEZs, a special economic zone that foreign traders could operate in under certain rules dictated by the current local ruler. Excavations prove that there was a settlement of foreigners who lived separate from the locals.

How did such a thriving port vanish from the pages of history? Possible clues lie in the 21st century. In December 2004, Pondicherry, along with a number of India's east coast towns were hit by the devastating tsunami. And more recently Cyclone Thane hit this coast. What little was left of the excavations at Arikamedu were damaged irreparably. Maybe it was such a series of tsunamis that emptied out this port in the medieval period. There are historical references to a massive tsunami in the 13th century. So only more excavations can answer this question.

Did the Romans know the sea route to India in 50 BCE, 1,500 years before Vasco da Gama?

No, the Romans didn't need to. Remember the story of Antony and Cleopatra? At the height of their power,

Egypt was a Roman province, so the Romans had land access to Indian Ocean ports. And they were terrifically advanced when it came to ship building. While the Arabs waited for the south-west monsoon to get over and later the north-east returning winds to subside before setting off to sea, the Romans did the reverse. Their strong ships allowed them to sail out during the monsoons, in fact, riding piggy back on the strong monsoon winds, arriving in India at high speed. They'd land in India's west coast ports of Barouch in Gujarat and at Muzaris in Kerala, before carrying on around Sri Lanka, to Arikamedu.

Chapter 17

The fact that Mathur Sir hadn't reappeared for some time to check on their progress, made Apu uneasy. 'I'd be much happier if he came and gave us a good yelling…not knowing what he's going to do is unnerving, somehow,' he said.

Apu's nervousness was contagious. So Nina, who had got lost in the South China Sea, reading up about Indian traders taking diamonds and pepper to China, slammed the fat encyclopaedia shut.

'Should we quickly do a king or two? The "People" notes we've got for Sir seem far less than our own notes.'

Apu thought a bit. He was enjoying discovering information about the sea-faring south Indian traders, who seemed far more adventurous than boring kings.

'Okay…but let's finish with these hot-shot traders, first,' he said.

The first 'East India Company' was Indian and existed 800 years before the English set up theirs!

Whenever 'East India Company' is mentioned, what first comes to mind is the British East India company, which was set up in 1600. Under a royal charter, it began to trade with India, and by 1803, it occupied and ruled over vast areas of our country, with an army that was double the size of the actual British Army. However, the British were actually late starters in the race towards the East. The Portuguese had already set up their 'State of India' or Estado da India by 1510 at Goa, and the Dutch had begun trading with India and even Indonesia, by the mid 1500s.

Yet we hardly know anything about the powerful, international Indian trading 'companies' or guilds

124 Kavitha Mandana

that operated along similar lines, centuries before the Europeans. From about 800 CE to the 1200s, there were a number of trade guilds that operated across south India. One of the most famous was the 'Five hundred swamis of Aihole' or Ainnurruvar. This network of traders operated across current-day Karnataka, Andhra, Telangana and Tamil Nadu. They began operations in Aihole, when the Chalukyas of Badami were ruling. And as the power structures changed and the Cholas became a dominant southern dynasty, the Aihole 500 moved further south and overseas, as Chola influence spread outside India. They specialized in protecting goods being transported over long distances, they offered logistical support and kept up good relations with kingdoms they traded in so that their consignments did not get held up at borders. They were known by different names in the various local languages.

They had their own flag, with the bull as their symbol. The Aihole 500 also had fortified trading posts across south India. They traded with China, Myanmar, Malaysia, Indonesia and Sri Lanka and had trading posts in many parts of South East Asia.

Inscriptions recording their activities date from the

earliest one found in Aihole dated 800 CE; to another found in Pudukottai in Tamil Nadu dated 927 CE; to one dated 1088, found in Barus, Sumatra. Records of the guild's activities have been found across Andhra and show that these powerful merchants built temples, maintained irrigation canals, lent money to kings, made long-term grants of their custom duties to particular temples and even had considerable influence on state policy.

During the heydays of the Chola dynasty, Rajendra Chola sent a naval expedition to South East Asia in 1025 CE, defeating a number of kingdoms. His victory inscriptions on the west wall of the Thanjavur temple boast of attacking and plundering Nicobar, parts of Malaysia (Kedah), the Srivijayas of Indonesia, etc. An inscription dated 1088 mentioning the Aihole 500 at Sumatra makes historians wonder—was the guild active in that region long before the Chola raid? In fact, historians like John Keay even wonder whether the Chola king was motivated by the Ainnurruvars to attack these kingdoms. Keay speculates that there could have been a number of reasons for this. South East Asian rulers who controlled the shipping lanes like the Straits of Malacca might have interfered with the Ainnurruvar's activities or harassed them.

Exporting elephants!

In his book *History of India*, Burton Stein translates a 1055 CE inscription about what the Aihole 500 did: 'By land routes and by water routes, penetrating into the regions of the six continents, with superior elephants, well-bred horses, large sapphires, moonstones, pearls, rubies, diamonds, cardamoms, cloves, sandal, camphor, musk, saffron and other perfumes and drugs...'

It seems that these merchants specialized in luxury and expensive goods. Also, trading in elephants probably meant close ties with royalty, because elephants were typically the property of kings or temples.

Though there are copper inscriptions about this guild dating from as late as the 1500s, as the big powerful kingdoms of the south got fragmented, the guilds seem to have disintegrated. Some other guilds did operate across the region even when the Europeans arrived, but when the British turned from traders into rulers, Indian guilds lost the power they once had.

Valiant merchants

The five hundred lords of Aihole were also referred to 'veerabalanja' or valiant merchants. And they lived by their own code of conduct—veerabalanja dharma. When we read about orthodox Indians' attitude towards foreign travel during the 1700s and 1800s, it's all about not crossing the ocean, because you could be excommunicated by your caste or community.

But Indians seem to have been far less orthodox and more open-minded in the preceding centuries. While the membership of some trade guilds was based on religion or a particular region, the Aihole 500 or the Ainnurruvar were made up of people cutting across regions and sects; many were also from outside the country. And they crossed the oceans as they built up strong trade networks across South East Asia. They were also the main channel through which Indian culture spread across Indonesia, Malaysia and Cambodia.

Chapter 18

'These are the kind of people Sir calls "useless"!' Nina giggled as she and Apu excitedly read up on the story of how the British smuggled tea plants out of China, in order to try starting their own plantations in India.

'We have to keep these guys hidden from him!' Apu replied. His fascination for the undercover agent tasked with stealing tea manufacturing secrets increased, just thinking of how Sir would frown upon them.

The story of how tea came to India is as strange as strange can be
⊙∽∾⊚

Ever since Vasco da Gama discovered the sea route

to India, European traders flooded the East, setting up trading posts across Indian, Chinese, Javanese and Japanese ports. From China, these European ships brought back tea, silk and porcelain and Europeans got addicted to all three. The Chinese emperor, though weak militarily, was smart enough to realize that tea-making and porcelain manufacture needed to be kept a secret. So any Chinese teaching foreigners how to grow tea, make porcelain or even speak local languages was sentenced to death. Further precautions included foreign ships being permitted to dock at only one port—Canton. From there they traded with local Chinese companies. Foreigners could not cross beyond the land boundary of the city.

The drink that started a war of independence

For years, the British East India Company loaded up its ships at Canton, unloaded some of the tea at Calcutta, Bombay and Madras for Indian consumption, and took the rest to Europe and even America, which was then a British colony. The English king had given the Company monopoly rights on the tea trade, so the Company could sell it at very high rates, earning large profits. It was this high tea tax that set off the American Revolution. American freedom fighters dumped the tea waiting to be unloaded from British ships into the waters of Boston harbour, and the war for independence began. By 1777, America was no longer a British colony.

Now, apart from the British government losing the high tax revenue from America, English merchant ships too lost out. By the 1840s, the Americans built super-fast sailing ships called clippers that raced to China, and returned loaded with precious tea. They did this in half the time that the old English East Indiamen (what the outdated ships of the company were called) managed.

Worse still, the Dutch East India company had beaten the English in the James Bond department. From their colony in Java, they'd sneaked into China, stolen plants and technology and set up a tea plantation in Indonesia. By 1829, the first Dutch-grown tea arrived by ship at Amsterdam.

Mission impossible?

In 1842, Robert Fortune, a botanist from the University of Edinburgh, Scotland vanished into Mainland China. He dressed himself in long robes and the wide brimmed hat of the Chinese, and probably even wore a 'ponytail' wig like the Mandarins. He concealed himself in a palanquin and travelled without a passport in areas that foreigners were banned from entering. The British East India Company desperately wanted to break China's complete monopoly of world tea supplies so they had hired Fortune to steal some trade secrets.

He was expected to steal precious tea plants and spy on how black tea was manufactured. Initially, his expedition was considered a grand success. He managed to smuggle out about 3,000 tea saplings along with a number of workers who knew all about tea production. The East India Company immediately set about growing these plants in Assam, India. But within months, all the saplings died. It looked like England would lose the Tea Race.

Luckily for them, much earlier in the 1820s, another Scotsman called Robert Bruce had gone exploring into the Assam jungles. Bruce had spent years living with

Kavitha Mandana

the local tribes, studying their customs and food habits. He discovered that they grew their own variety of tea. But when he tried telling executives from the East India Company about this, they ignored him. It was only in the late 1840s, when Fortune's 3,000 saplings had all died, and Robert Bruce himself had died, that his brother Charles Bruce was able to convince the English to give Assam tea a chance.

After studying the plant and savouring the tea, the British went into overdrive. Thousands of Indians were hired overnight to clear the jungle and plant tea. In the mad rush to win the Tea Race, British used military-like techniques to get a quick tea crop. Of the thousands of hired labourers a third died in the Assam jungles: some from rampant malaria, some on account of the inhuman working conditions and many shot at when they tried to escape—like they were 'army deserters running away from battle'. When the first eight crates of Assam tea arrived by ship at the London auctions, it was called the 'bitter brew'—grown at the cost of so many Indian lives.

As tea planting and manufacturing spread across Assam, the British began experimenting in other parts of India. The Assam saplings grown in the Darjeeling hills proved to be a huge success. The higher altitude and the drier climate resulted in tea with a very different flavour. Soon Darjeeling teas became the favourite of connoisseurs, and even today command the highest prices at tea auctions.

James Bond Version 2.0

In the 1870s, the English got a taste of their own medicine. Prince Muhammed Mirza arrived in India as a diplomat from the Persian court. This prince, also called Kashef el Sultaneh, rather liked his tea. Thanks to the overland Silk Route from China, the people of Central Asia and the Middle East had all gotten hooked onto tea long before the Europeans did. But this prince was smart. He knew that the British would never allow him to legally transfer tea plants from India and set up production units in Persia. In 1857—the same year as India's first War of Independence—the Persians and British had fought a minor war, and there was an uneasy truce between the two countries.

Prince Kashef had been educated in Paris, so taking a page out of Robert Fortune's James Bond manual, he disguised himself as a French businessman, travelled through Assam and managed to smuggle about 3,000 saplings out of British India, via the Kangra valley. There are rumours that his diplomatic immunity allowed his baggage to go unchecked at the borders.

By 1882, Prince Kashef had successfully set up a tea plantation close to the Caspian Sea. The prince's tomb at Lahijan is today a tea museum, and across two states in Iran—Gilan and Mazundaran—there are 32,000 hectares under tea cultivation.

Chapter 19

'Do you think what men wore centuries ago, would interest Sir?' Apu asked, flipping through a book on traditional textiles of India.

'Why not? Men are people, right?' Nina said and they both laughed.

She added, 'Maybe if you link what men wore to some king or emperor, it would be okay? You know how he's only interested in royalty.'

'And in height-weight-length measurements,' Apu added, in a slightly disgruntled fashion.

'Hey! We can do men's fashion, and begin with the jodhpurs…it's clearly linked to royalty!' Nina sat up excitedly. 'And there are loads of measurements involved, too!'

'I hope you're not making this up as we go along?' Apu asked, worriedly.

'No, I'm serious! In the 1890s, there was this totally

posh polo-playing Rajput prince called Sir Pratap Singh,' Nina began.

'Listen, I'm not dumb...posh polo-playing Prince Pratap? You think I'm going to fall for this made-up story of yours?' Apu sneered.

It required Nina to pull out the book on the royal families of Rajasthan to convince Apu that such a prince did indeed exist. He was the regent of Jodhpur. And because he found British breeches and Indian traditional men's wear uncomfortable for long hours of polo-playing, he designed his own trousers for horse-riding. These became well known as jodhpurs.

'And just because some prince got hold of a local tailor to stitch his riding pants, the whole world blindly followed him?' Apu asked, incredulously.

'No...he was lucky, because he got to show off his riding pants on the biggest stage ever,' Nina said. 'In 1897, during Queen Victoria's Diamond Jubilee celebrations in England, he and his Rajput polo team were kitted out in "jodhpurs" and their team won most of the matches they played.'

'Maybe if his team had lost, nobody would have been interested in his balloony pants,' Apu added.

So, confident that Sir Pratap Singh would keep Mathur Sir happy, the two collected what today look like rather odd men's fashion trends followed centuries ago.

Ancient men's fashion was quite strange!

There were some strange things going on in the fashion world centuries ago. To begin with, for a long time, men's and women's wardrobes were very similar! From the early days of the Mauryas to the Gupta era, both men and women wore an unstitched version of the dhoti that typically reached just below the knees. This was called the antariya. Men and women then used another length of fabric called the kayabandhan to hold the antariya in place. The difference here would be that the woman's kayabandhan could be embellished with strings of pearls or beads. They both wore an upper covering, a cotton dupatta-like fabric called the uttariya. Men and women wore earrings, necklaces and bracelets. Men too grew their hair long. I wonder what their fashion magazines would have looked like!

Of course, other fashions were also followed. And as more people migrated into India, because of trade or through conquest, wardrobes changed. The Central Asian Kushans, who ruled northern India from about 50 CE to 230 CE and whose greatest king was Kanishka, wore high boots, long warm coats and trousers that kept the wearers warm through severe winters. So Indian styles changed to experiment with these new wardrobes.

Indian men probably were the first to wear high heels!

When Alexander came charging across the Asian continent with his army, his close buddies included many Greeks who fancied themselves as writers. One of them was Nearchus, who also wrote about his travels in India. He's also known as Admiral Nearchus by the

Greeks, mainly because he partly financed the building of a fleet of boats, which he then used to sail back to the Persian Gulf.

He described Indian menswear fairly accurately—white cotton antariyas, uttariyas, and parasols as protection against the hot Indian sun. He also said, '…they wear shoes made of white leather and these are elaborately trimmed, while the soles are variegated and made of great thickness, to make the wearer seem so much taller.'

Other height-gaining hacks

There were other tricks used by Indian men to appear taller—the main one was the turban. It certainly adds many inches to a man's height, and by the Gupta era itself, the turban had become the most important part of a man's wardrobe. The colour, design and how it was tied displayed the man's lineage, the region he came from, his religion and his status.

If you've watched your mother folding up her sari, she's handling six and half metres of cloth. If you happen to be Maharashtrian, your mum's sari could measure nine yards (8.22 metres).

Now imagine your father in your mother's shoes…I don't mean, 'Imagine your father trying on a six-and-half-metre sari.' Just try imagining him having to wear a turban using 25 metres of cotton fabric! That's about four times the length of a sari and would need various members of the family to hold up the cloth as it zig-zagged through all the rooms of your home at folding-up time. Just for your information, 25 metres is about 80+ feet.

Rajput noblemen from the pre-independence era took the easy way out—they hired the 'pagri bandh', a professional turban tier, who would twirl, twist and wind those 25 metres of fabric around a man's head in such a way that from a distance of 100 feet, anyone would be able to tell his status, caste, religion and regional background. And of course 25 metres on your head will also make you look considerably taller.

Royal fashions

Fashion was taken very seriously by kings and emperors. Humayun, the Mughal emperor, who was also an astronomer, wore different coloured clothes based on the phases of the moon and the positions of the planet. Before him, the Chalukyan king, Someshwara (1124-35) wrote that he himself only wore light-coloured clothes in spring; pure white billowing cotton in summer; red-, brown- and rose-coloured clothes during the monsoon and saffron-coloured wool in winter.

The 'white billowing cotton' and other local fashions certainly confused one famous writer new to India. In the 11th century, during the Sultanate period, Al-Biruni wrote, 'They use turbans for trousers...wear trousers lined with as much cotton as would suffice to make a number of counterpanes and saddle rugs...'

Kavitha Mandana

Chapter 20

Nina and Apu had handed in the rest of their assignment to Mathur Sir. They were now free to breathe the dusty air of the school playground at lunch break, and really, there was no longer any need for them to hang out at the library. But they found they could not stay away. They just had to follow up the last few leads they'd picked up in history books. Now, no longer bothered by Sir's threats of punishments, they discovered that snooping through history could be super cool.

The librarian smiled when they entered. These two had been bitten by the history bug. What had begun as a punishment, would now become an addiction. It had happened to her, so she recognized the signs. And it happened to students regularly at the school, too—maybe once every two years.

'Your first lot of notes are with the Principal,' she said casually as the two walked past her.

They both stopped in their tracks. Nina had given up on those notes Sir grabbed that day, sure he'd destroyed them. What would Principal Ma'am do with them, she wondered.

'Are we back in trouble, now?' Apu groaned. Just when he thought they were clear of all Social Studies related crimes…now *this*.

The librarian refused to tell them anything more, so they just drowned their worries in history. Here's what they found.

A 43-verSe poem praising garlic certainly SoundS weird!

Bower, another undercover agent?

It was the year that British India signed a border treaty with the Chinese Qing dynasty, demarcating the boundaries between India, Bhutan and Tibet. That might explain why, in 1890, Hamilton Bower, from British military intelligence was lurking about in Chinese Turkestan. There are no valuable cash crops or minerals in this cold desert across the Hindu Kush mountains, north of Kashmir, that could have interested the British Empire.

Perhaps Bower came back with some strategic secrets, but he became famous for buying (for a bargain!) a set of birch-bark manuscripts discovered in a sand-covered, abandoned Buddhist monastery in Kuchar. The dry, arid climate of the freezing desert had preserved this set of manuscripts for almost 1,500 years!

When Bower sent the manuscripts to the Asiatic Society of Bengal, there was much excitement. This was now the oldest surviving original manuscript from India's past. It was also the earliest to mention Ayurvedic formulae.

Palaeographists got to work, dating the document. A.F. Rudolf Hoernle, a Sanskrit scholar and well-known Indologist, was the one who eventually translated the entire manuscript. He gauged that this Sanskrit text, written in Gupta-era Brahmi script (with some Prakrit thrown in), dated from about 300 CE. Later research (done in the 1980s) has dated the book from the first half of 500 CE.

The birch-bark manuscript has 'pages' somewhat like palm-leaf books, with a hole in the page through which a metal wire or twine is passed through. The set is made up of seven separately paginated booklets. The most valuable part is the first three booklets that are on Ayurvedic medicine. It is this section that has a 43-verse poem on garlic!

Of course, it would be unfair to imagine some poet, smitten by garlic, gazing into the horizon as he wrote about his strange love. In ancient India, even science and medical texts were written in verse as this made it easier to memorize them. Knowledge was only rarely written down, and few original manuscripts survived India's damp monsoons. But committed to memory, parents passed on their knowledge to their children, teachers did the same with students and priests with novices.

This particular text lists out all the benefits of garlic, which are many—even modern medicine ranks it as one of the super-foods. Interestingly, Brahmin priests avoided garlic on account of certain properties such as helping you stay young and fit, etc. But the Bower manuscript suggests that priests could enjoy the medicinal properties of garlic by first feeding it to the cows and drinking that milk!

Hoernle's commitment to ancient medicine

After releasing a quick translation of parts of the text in 1891, Hoernle spent the years 1893-1897 doing a thorough translation and getting the manuscript ready for publication. In 1909, he redid the medical texts with more notes and comparisons from other surviving texts on Ayurveda. Hoernle got to know the texts so well that he identified about four different authors of the manuscript, and he even guessed which part of the Gupta empire each of them came from—just from their writing styles!

Another chapter in the Bower set is about the mantra to chant when a person is afflicted by snake bite. Like the Ayurvedic medical formulations that are presented in verse form, this mantra is presented within a story, involving the Buddha himself and his favourite cousin and disciple, Ananda.

In Rudolf Hoernle's annotations to his translation, he points out that this was very clearly a Buddhist text. So medical recipes that might be recorded by a Hindu writer as 'Narayana's cure' in some other book, would appear here as 'Siddharta's cure'. And while mentioning in verse how a particular drug acts on the body, the text will add something like, '…gets rid of all diseases, just as The Enlightened One got rid of all distractions.'

Cubo-crazy?

Did you know that in ancient India, astrologers practiced something called cubomancy? This was about predicting the future based on how you throw the dice (the cube)! People wanting to know about their future would throw the dice three times, and all three numbers were recorded in the correct sequence. Each number combination had a name. The Bower manuscript has ready lists on what each set of numbers mean.

Be careful not to throw this combination with the dice:

'The third karna: 4 1 1: Thou meditates going on a journey, but thou wilt meet with misfortune; thou wilt return with thy business unfinished; there is no doubt about it.'

How about this, another number combination that you better not throw:

'The second karna: 1 4 1: By the act of god, thy whole property has been destroyed…'

But there are more of the positive variety. Go ahead and roll the dice. You could get:

'The first sakti: 3 4 1: Thou art planning a marriage and thou wilt soon accomplish it, and obtain an affectionate relative who will bestow on thee wealth and pleasure.'

Or:

'The third vahula: 4 8 3: Manifold, I see, is thy business and thou possessest many sons; look forward to thy own happiness, thou wilt obtain all that belongs to it.'

The National Mission for Manuscripts

In 2003, the Indian government launched the National Mission for Manuscripts (NAMAMI), across all states. What this meant was, any person or institution that had old manuscripts, could bring them across to manuscript centres set up in all the states. Here, help would be given on restoring the manuscripts if needed and digital copies of the contents would be made. Owners of the manuscripts could then take them back. In this way, even if those manuscripts got lost due to flood, fire or theft, a digital copy would still be saved and remain accessible to researchers and scholars.

Manuscripts in India are on copper plates, on the barks of various kinds of trees, on palm leaf and even on cloth. Monks in the Karnataka region smeared a paste made of coal and tamarind seed onto cloth. This gave it a stiff black base on which monks did their weekly accounts using limestone as chalk.

To prevent insects from feeding off the manuscripts, dried neem, tulsi and tobacco were sprinkled around

Kavitha Mandana

where manuscripts are stored. From across India, surprises have emerged as the Mission rolled out.

* From Majuli (Assam), the world's largest inhabited river island on the Brahmaputra, one of the Vaishnavi monasteries (the Auniati Satra) brought a veterinary book on elephant medicine to be digitized— the *Hasti Vidyarnava*!

* While Hindi, Sanskrit and Odiya rank the highest in language manuscripts, Tibetan books outnumbered Tamil, Kannada and Telugu. This is because of the Dalai Lama's presence in Himachal Pradesh, and the large Tibetan refugee population in the state.

Chapter 21

In class, Mathur Sir glared over his glasses at Apu sitting slouched over his desk, and barked, 'Stand up, you over there!'

Without even looking up, Apu knew that 'you' meant himself. He stood up.

'I went through your notes…where is that other clumsy one, breaking models?'

Nina shot up and protested, 'Sir, I didn't break…'

Sir waved her aside, silencing her. 'Leave that now. If I had to grade your punishment, I would have given it a B.'

Nina and Apu stared at him. B? Getting a 'B' from Mathur Sir was like receiving a Ph.D! Relieved, they both sat down, Sir having turned to the blackboard where he was scribbling a series of dates.

That lunch break at the library, they were so lost in Sir's 'B' grading, they forgot to ask the librarian about what their notes were still doing in the Principal's office. Instead, free from Mathur Sir's height-weight details, they went romping across centuries, and across continents looking at how colonialism changed the way we all lived.

The travelling potato

Every October, the British celebrate National Curry Week! When we sent the British packing home in 1947, our return gift seems to have been the Indian curry. It's now almost a national dish across the UK, with thousands of Indian, Bangladeshi and Pakistani restaurants serving South Asian cuisine, not just to Asian immigrants but to the English themselves.

A global khichdi

In the same way, a lot of what we believe is typically 'Indian' has come to our dining tables from across the world. Over the past 1,000 years, the Turks, Afghans and Mughals introduced us to kebabs, naans, rotis, khichdi and biriyani. It was the British who first got hooked to tea, a Chinese drink, and then introduced us Indians to it. The Chinese also gave us soya beans, litchis and a number of berries. But it's the Portuguese that our taste buds need to be most grateful to.

The Spanish and Portuguese were the first to begin colonizing the Americas. Vasco da Gama was sent off by the ambitious Portuguese Prince Phillip to find 'the Indies' and he discovered the sea route to India. The Portuguese presence in India grew after this, while doing trade with the Indians. And crops discovered in South America soon found their way to Europe and then to India.

Potatoes had been cultivated by the Incas in Peru since 5000 BCE. Portuguese ships brought this easy-to-grow tuber back to Europe, where it revolutionized agriculture. And from there, they shipped it to India, where the British set up the first potato farms in Dehra

Dun. Aloo tikki from the north of India and puri-palya from the south are favourite everyday foods in India today. So every time you bite into a hot potato cutlet on a cold winter day, send up a quiet 'thank-you' to Vasco da Gama.

Tomatoes grew only in Mexico, but by the 16th century, they were popular in Europe, and cultivation began in India by the 1850s—but only because the English liked the vegetable. Indians hadn't yet taken to it. Along with these two favourites, the Portuguese brought capsicum, corn, papaya, pineapple, avocado, sapota and cashew. And if Indians cannot imagine a life without rajma-chawal…well rajma, the India name given to kidney beans, came to us from Mexico and Guatemala.

Not every plant or crop the Portuguese introduced here was good, though. It was they who brought tobacco to India during Mughal times. But they're forgiven, because they also packed their ships with chilli from South America!

Those of us who can't begin their day without filter coffee need to be reminded that this heady brew came to us from Yemen and Ethiopia, along with Arab traders.

It was Baba Budan who planted the first bushes in the Bababudangiri hills in Chikmagalur, in Karnataka.

How old is curry-and-rice?

Of course, there's a lot in our diet that's purely local. In fact, the curry and rice combination is probably the oldest continuously prepared recipe anywhere in the world. During excavations in an Indus Valley-era town called Farmana, east of Delhi, while analyzing the teeth of the skeletons that the archaeologists had found, traces of turmeric and ginger were discovered along with rice husk—suggesting that the last meal of that person was probably curry and rice. Findings at this site have been dated to 2500–2000 BCE.

Pepper, the Black Gold, loses its sheen

For centuries, Indian spices only reached Europe with the Arab traders as the middlemen. Arab ships sailed to India's west coast, where they stocked up on all that the Middle East and Europe wanted. Kerala was the only place where pepper was grown and it was so precious, it was sometimes used as currency. From the Persian Gulf, Indian spices and textiles travelled overland on caravans to the Mediterranean coast, and then onto Europe's capitals. But as the Spanish and Portuguese got better at navigation, and more confident after their discovery of the Americas, they soon discovered the sea route to the East.

This disrupted the spice trade in many ways. The Europeans soon replaced the Arab traders, cutting them out of the business, and while arriving here as traders themselves, they went on to become colonists.

By introducing chillies to India, the local demand for pepper now dropped. Curries no longer needed expensive pepper to spice them up. Chillies were soon grown all over India, adding a new flavour to our cuisine.

Chapter 22

Over the past few weeks of hectic reading, Apu had marvelled at how trade and colonialism had changed the world so much.

'It's not just food, which I think got much tastier with all the mixing of crops from across the world—but even fashions and interior decoration styles changed,' Apu said.

Nina glared at him for sounding so cheery. She'd started out collecting words like 'verandah' and 'bungalow' that the English had borrowed from Hindi. But then stumbled across other words and names that revealed some uncomfortable truths. She particularly got irritated by words like 'chintz'.

'I can't understand why a word like that should bother you!' Apu snorted.

'That's because you don't know it's history!' Nina snapped back. And before Apu could retort she continued, 'Chintz was actually the English pronunciation of the Hindustani "chint" for a glazed cotton with floral block-prints.'

And before Apu could butt in, she went on, 'It got so popular in Europe that they imported millions of pieces of this fabric from India. English and French mill owners panicked...and both France and Britain banned its import during the mid 1700s.'

'So? That sounds like a typical trade war,' Apu said, still wondering what Nina was bothered about.

'It was more than that,' Nina said. 'During the ban, the English and French mills learned to replicate and copy our fabric...and worse, today, the word "chintz" is associated with a look that's typically English! Doesn't that irritate you?'

Finally, it made sense to Apu. He'd never dreamt that words hid so many layers of history.

Words have weird layers that can be peeled off!

The brain fever bird?

Reading books written by the British during the Raj, readers often come across this strange creature called the Brain Fever Bird! To the English, the bird's call sounded like 'brain fever' being repeated over and over again. In one bestseller from the 1930s, *100 Days of Lt. Ian MacHorton,* which is supposed to be the true story of a British soldier fighting the Japanese army in the forests of the North East and Burma, this bird's call almost drove the author mad.

But this supposedly crazy and maddening bird is none other than the much-loved papiha. Indians love the bird and its lilting song. Along with the peacock, the papiha is associated with the coming of rain, and

Kavitha Mandana

hence the associations are happy and filled with hope. Indians are so fond of this bird, that it's quite a common name given to baby girls. The Sanskrit name datyuha (dadatyanandamdatyuha) translates to 'giving joy' or 'exhilarating'.

Its zoological name is Common Hawk-Cuckoo, and like its other cousins, this bird too is a brood parasite, laying its eggs in other birds' nests and leaving the parenting tasks to that poor 'other mother'. Strange, how one culture hears music in a bird's call and another finds it infuriating.

The world's highest peak gets renamed

Mount Everest is another name that conceals layers of history. To begin with, Mount Everest wasn't 'discovered' by the British. Located close to today's border between Nepal and Tibet, the mountain already had two beautiful names. For centuries, the Nepalese referred to it as Sagarmatha and the Tibetians called it Chomolungma.

In 1847, when employees of the British Survey of India spotted the peak in the Himalayas from across the mountains, they had no idea about it, so it was 'named' most unimaginatively as Peak XV! At that time, Sir George Everest was the Surveyor General of India. And since the British had begun measuring the length and breadth of this vast colony that they'd acquired in what came to be known as the Great Trignometric Survey, Everest had gone looking for a good mathematician. He needed someone with a talent for spherical trigonometry. Soon, based on the recommendation of the Hindu College (Calcutta) Principal, nineteen-year-old Radhanath Sidkar joined the Survey of India. His outstanding genius led to the discovery of many new methods to make accurate measurements. Throughout his career, he remained the Survey's key 'computer'— his brain doing the number crunching that is done by today's high-performance computers.

Once Peak XV had been spotted, Radhanath got to work, using spherical trigonometry to measure the true height of the mountain. After four years of number-crunching, in 1852, he burst into the Dehra Dun office of the new Surveyor General, Andrew Waugh. He excitedly confirmed that Peak XV was the highest peak in the world—29,002 feet (today, a 150 years later, Everest is 29,029 feet, since its height has been increasing by 4 millimetres every year). By then, Sir George Everest, a vocal admirer of Radhanath, had retired. And Waugh wasn't as certain as his predecessor about this 'native' mathematician's talents. He did the safe thing. He decided to first name the mountain. Even here, he differed from Everest who believed that if there was a local name for a mountain, peak or river, that name ought to remain. He decided to avoid Sagarmatha and Chomolungma in favour of Mount Everest.

It was only in 1856, four years after a series of other British and European experts reconfirmed that the 39-year-old Radhanath's calculations were indeed correct, was it announced to the world that 'the British had discovered the highest peak in the world'! Almost a century later, long after the British had left the subcontinent, Mount Everest was scaled for the first time by the Nepalese mountaineer Tenzing Norgay and the New Zealander, Edmund Hillary, on 29 May 1953.

It was the day of the current British queen Elizabeth's coronation, and the Western press breathlessly reported about this event as a 'gift to the Queen on such an important day'. It is indeed strange how a Nepalese and a New Zealander scaling a peak in free Nepal can be viewed as a gift to the English queen! It's probably because of the name that the English still felt a sense of ownership of a peak they'd renamed Everest.

In 1960, the Nepalese government decided to give the mountain its old name back, calling it Sagarmatha again.

Names that carry the pre-English colonial imprint

Peel off layers from some other names and more hidden history gets revealed. The coastal town of Tranquebar in Tamil Nadu was really an old town called Tharangambadi. When all of Europe was rushing to the East looking for their own spice routes, Denmark set up a trading post and Christian mission at Tharangambadi. Of course the Dutch were already busy on the west coast in Cochin, from where they traded, having pushed the Portuguese out.

If you ever wondered how among the cluster of ancient cave temples in western India—Ajanta, Ellora and Kanheri—there is one called 'Elephanta', it was the

Kavitha Mandana

Portuguese at work. Before they arrived, the island with these caves was called Gharipuri, and its outstanding attraction was the massive statue of Sadashiva (three-headed Shiva). But because the landing stage at the island had an elephant statue, the Portuguese named the island Elephante. And in their attempt to stamp out Hinduism, they defaced many statues and carvings in the Gharipuri caves. In spite of this, these cave temples of the Gupta period, mainly dedicated to Shiva and dating back 1,500 years, are today a UNESCO World Heritage site.

Other cave temples did not survive so well. Kanheri, a Mauryan-era Buddhist chaitya, was defaced very badly and turned into St Celicia's Chapel, while the Portuguese priests also ran an orphanage and a seminary within these caves.

When victors use words to erase the vanquished

One of the worst aspects of the English colonizing India was how they destroyed India's ancient textile traditions. Typically, Indian farmers had looms at home. When the harvest or planting season was over, weaving was a good way to earn extra money. And when the monsoons failed, or too much rain destroyed a crop, farmers rarely starved because they always used their looms to earn themselves a non-agricultural income. But the British taxed Indian textiles so highly that Indians could no longer afford their own cloth, and were forced to buy cheap cloth manufactured in British factories in England. Millions of Indians across the country were forced to abandon their looms. Later, during the tragic Bengal Famine during the World War II, between 3-4 million Indians died of starvation, something that would never have happened had the handloom industry not also been killed by the British.

Paisley: This was a textile town in Scotland, where they practiced how to copy the Kashmiri shawl. Cashmere wool, made from goat's hair, was very popular in England, and to cater to the high demand for it, in Paisley they began weaving these shawls using sheep's wool. The main motif or design woven into the shawl was the curved tear-drop that originated in Iran. In India it is sometimes taken to represent the mango. With the looms in Paisley mass producing 'Kashmiri shawls', that famous design motif from the East was renamed the Paisley motif—erasing its ancient history.

Chapter 23

It was probably going to be one of their last lunch breaks in the library since the quarterly exams were to begin soon. Nina said, 'I think, I'm a bit saturated with the past. I want to read a good science fiction novel.'

But when Apu came across an article called 'The Annual Beetle Harvest in the Arakans' they were both hooked, retracing their way back into the pages of history. Though Nina was a bit grossed out by the thought of collecting thousands of dead beetles ('Did they smell?' she wondered) she couldn't take her eyes off the page.

Apu started to laugh, 'What crazy lengths people go to, just to be fashionable,' he marvelled.

'And not just us Indians...look,' she pointed out some pictures on a page, 'People in ancient Egypt, Japan and Victorian England also went through a phase of beetle-mania!' she said.

No.1 oddball fashion trend?
Beetle embroidery!

The beetle hunt

For centuries, every year during the monsoons, beetle harvesters trudged off into the hardwood forests of the Arakan mountains looking for beetles. This remote region along the Bay of Bengal falls in present-day Myanmar. Thankfully, there was no 'animal-cruelty' involved in this hunt because by the time they began their harvesting, the forests were flooded with millions of beetles that were already dead. The harvesters wanted only one particular type of beetle of the genus sternocera. These were much in demand across India, Burma (Myanmar), China, Japan and Thailand because of the beautiful emerald green iridescent colouring of their wing casings.

The wood-boring beetles swarmed the forests, mated and then died—all within a period of just three to four weeks. Once collected, this harvest would be dispatched to cities in Bengal. Later, after the British arrived, Calcutta became the nodal hub in the beetle trade. From there they would get distributed to Jaipur and other well-known centres of embroidery.

This beetle's wing cases (called elytra) protected the delicate flight wings and provided aerodynamic 'lift' when spread. The metallic sheen and durability of the wing case made it popular as the 'sequins' of medieval times. Either the entire wing case was used in embroidery or the casing was cut into smaller pieces, which were then sewn onto silk or muslin, along with beads, gold thread and other embellishments. Of course, this was a luxury, so such embroidery was mostly for royal families and courtiers. It was very popular in the Jaipur court, and this city's embroiderers became adept at their craft. From here, beetle mania then spread to all parts of India.

Beetle fashions across the world

For certain Naga tribes of the North East, wearing beetle wings was a status symbol. Beetles worn as accessories is a practice that goes back thousands of years. The Pharaohs of ancient Egypt considered the dung or scarab beetle sacred. The royals had scarabs carved out of metal or moulded in clay, and common people had real dead beetles 'mummified' in transparent resin. When this dried, it became a beetle-pendant, to be worn as a sacred and good-luck charm.

According to some historians, women from India and Sri Lanka went a step further. They even 'wore' live beetles. Coppery green live Chrysora ocellate beetles, about an inch-and-a-half in length, were worn as ornaments during festive occasions. And to prevent them from flying away, one of their legs was leashed to the woman's clothes by a minute chain!

Beetles crawl into Victorian hairstyles

Like other handicrafts from India such as kalamkari and Kashmir's pashmina shawls, beetle-craft soon became a trend in Victorian England too. Some enterprising businessman had a beautiful Western-style gown of the latest fashion embroidered with beetle wings by Indian craftsmen. He displayed this at the Great Exhibition of 1851 (which was held in London's Hyde Park). This expo, the largest of its kind in the world, attracted millions of visitors. As a result, beetle wings became the rage in the West. And along with adorning their flamboyant hats with feathers of exotic birds (and in some cases, even the entire bird!) European women also adopted the trend of tethering live beetles to their ensembles.

Beetle-wing casings have been so durable that examples of such embroidery have survived for centuries. Even when the fabric has begun to disintegrate, the beetle wings have not. Examples of well-preserved beetle-wing embroidery exist across India in the textile museums and ancestral collections of the old royal families and even in museums across the West, including the Victoria and Albert Museum, London.

The beetle-wing temple in Japan

In India, beetle wings were sewn onto clothes worn by both men and women. But since fabric deteriorates over the years, it is difficult to date how old the practice of beetle-wing decoration is. The wings were also used to embellish miniature paintings and other objects of art in Mughal and Rajput courts, where karkhanas or royal workshops for artists churned out fine craft-work for the elite.

And there is proof that in Japan, too, beetle wings were considered an art material as early as 850 CE. In the ancient Japanese capital of Nara, outside the famous Buddhist Horyu-ji temple is the Tamamushi shrine. 'Tamamushi' is the Japanese word for 'jewel beetle'. So though there is little evidence of the beetle wings that encrusted the outer part of this shrine, the temple records reveal that this tiny shrine that held sacred Buddhist texts was once covered with beautiful beetle wings.

Lady Macbeth's gown

From exporting beetle-wing embroidered fabric and ready-made gowns, India soon began exporting beetle wings itself. European designers were eager to use the jewel-like elytra in their own creations. One such design became world famous in 1888.

Kavitha Mandana

Macbeth, one of Shakespeare's most famous plays, has been performed for centuries. In Victorian England, when the British Empire was at its peak, and before movies had been invented, theatre was very popular. Ellen Terry was a popular stage actress of her time. In 1888, when she performed the role of Lady Macbeth, she was immortalized. Partly for her great acting skills, but also because of what she wore—a beetle-wing green gown! During the time the play ran in London, the sea-green crocheted gown with thousands of beetle-wing cases sewn on, became a sensation. A well-known artist, John Singer Sargent, painted Ellen Terry in this costume, making it the most memorable stage costume of its time.

The play ran for six months non-stop. Ellen Terry even acted the part on stages across the US, so when she finally donated all her costumes to a trust, the gown was in tatters. In 2011, with donations amounting to £110,000 and a thousand new beetle wings, and after a period of almost five years, Lady Macbeth's gown was restored for public display.

Chapter 24

'Here, take a look at this magazine, you both might like it,' the librarian said, as Apu dashed past her. He knew that with exams the following week, and having missed all his football practices over the past month, this would be his last hour in the library. There were so many historical leads that he wanted to follow up, just for fun…but he wondered if he'd have enough time.

He grabbed the magazine and ran on, tossing it at the table where Nina was scribbling away furiously. She looked relieved when she saw him and pushed her notebook across to him.

'Here, you finish this…all our notes on the topic are in that green diary…remember we researched this during that first week when we were only supposed to do ancient structures?' she asked as she massaged her palm that seemed stiff from all the writing.

Apu remembered. He sat down and picked up writing where Nina had left off...

Oddly enough, international maritime law is based on the principle of 'Finders, keepers'!

You must have heard the expression, 'Finders keepers; losers weepers'? It is typically used by cousins and friends when THEY find something YOU have lost, like a pen, a bar of chocolate or a book, which *they* keep, and *you* weep over! But what about treasure that is worth crores of rupees?

Reclaiming the S.S. Gairsoppa

In 2013, a Florida-based company called Odyssey Marine Exploration went down 3 miles deep into the

North Atlantic Ocean to unearth tonnes of silver from a sunken ship. The firm had used the latest technology—GPS, sonar beams and remote-controlled underwater rovers—apart from old maps and a lot of time to track a particular shipwreck—that of the S.S. Gairsoppa that was travelling from Calcutta to the UK in 1941. World War II was raging and during the war, the British Government had requisitioned all private ships for war duty. So the S.S. Gairsoppa, a badly maintained vessel that normally travelled only in the Indian Ocean, had to now sail to the UK carrying 198 tonnes of silver and tea from Calcutta.

Since Britain was an island and required all its raw materials from overseas to feed its factories, the German strategy was to destroy ships sailing to Britain—that way it could starve British factories. German submarines called U-Boats waited in the stormy waters of the Atlantic Ocean to sink these ships. So as vessels neared Britain, they formed convoys and travelled under the escort of British warships. Unfortunately, S.S. Gairsoppa (that is the old name for Jog Falls) joined a convoy after leaving its last port in West Africa but developed problems and couldn't keep pace with the other ships. It trailed behind and was an easy target for a German sub that shot it down 300 miles off the Irish coast on 17 February 1941. All the crew and officers, except for one Englishman, died. Seventy Indian seamen, who had never faced the cold of the North Atlantic, were among those who drowned.

Years later, the UK government hired Odyssey to search for and raise the cargo. The deal signed BEFORE Odyssey began work was that the British government would get 20 per cent of the silver, and Odyssey would keep 80 per cent to cover its costs of exploration and salvage. International maritime law specifies that government property that goes down during any war remains the property of that government, even if it's sitting at the bottom of the sea. So in this case, the UK government claimed ownership of the silver. But technically, it didn't own ALL of it.

Who owns what's at the bottom of the sea?

Apparently, only 110 of the 198 tonnes of silver belonged to the British Army. The rest belonged to the British India Government, which gave up all its dominions and assets (as well as its debt!) to India and

Pakistan in August 1947. All British Indian assets were divided between India and Pakistan on a 82.5:17.5 ratio so the non-military 88 tonnes of silver which neither Odyssey nor the British government is talking about (and which today is probably worth more than Rs 1000 crores) could actually be claimed by India and Pakistan! And even Bangladesh, which got carved out of Pakistan. Of course, no one knows yet whether any of the South Asian countries thought of suing Odyssey like Spain did, but it is an interesting legal point to think about.

Odyssey vs. Spain

A couple of years earlier, Odyssey had searched for, found and raised the cargo of a Spanish ship off the coast of Portugal. The cargo of gold and silver was worth half a billion dollars and Odyssey believed that… well, finders were keepers and the losers weepers! But the Spanish government thought otherwise. Based on international maritime law, it sued Odyssey in the US courts. The ship whose wreck they had located had been blown up in 1803 by the British during wartime. So the US Supreme Court ruled that the gold and silver belonged to the Spanish government. Odyssey had to watch their carefully salvaged cargo being airlifted out of a US air base, back to Spain. Naturally, before they went looking for S.S. Gairsoppa, they first signed a deal with the British government on how much each party got to keep.

The company, Odyssey Maritime Exploration Inc, has also been accused by archaeologists across the world for being treasure hunters. On land, any ancient treasure found legally belongs to the government....to be studied by historians and kept for display in a state museum. But a lot of the old artefacts that Odyssey has found underwater is now up for sale on its website, instead of being viewed in a museum. After Odyssey found the wreck of S.S. Republic, a Civil War-era US vessel that sank off the American coast due to bad weather, American Civil War-era souvenirs could be bought off the Odyssey site. How about paying $1500 for an empty pickle bottle!

Think about it...should finders be keepers? Or should salvaged shipwreck cargo go to museums?

War debts

There are countless other unacknowledged debts that Britain owes its former colonies. The seventy Indian seamen who drowned on the S.S. Gairsoppa have been commemorated at the Chittagong War Memorial. Nearly 2 million Indians fought in World War II. And officially, 36,000 lost their lives fighting a war that began because of European rivalries (though everyone believes that South Asian war casualties were far higher). The 3 million plus people who died during the Bengal Famine (because Indian-grown grain was forcibly collected and sent to England to combat wartime shortages there) need to be counted as war casualties.

Indian soldiers played a crucial role during World War II in battles across Europe, in the Middle East, in North Africa, Burma and at sea. Yet, when the recent popular war movie *Dunkirk* was made, Asian critics slammed it because it was a 'white wash'. None of the battle scenes showed the true colours of those who fought against Hitler. Every European country had forced thousands of people from their colonies to fill its armies. North African soldiers from Algiers and other

French colonies fought on the side of the French, yet were absent onscreen. So were the Indians, Nepalis, Kenyans and other 'subjects of the British King'.

Marine archaeology

When private bounty hunters like Odyssey use GPS, satellite imagery and robotic equipment to locate sunken ships with treasure, governments need to step up. The National Institute of Oceanography in Goa works with the ASI, the Indian Navy and a host of other government institutes to study, record and preserve India's submerged cultural heritage. The NIO's work began in the 1970s, while the ASI set up the UAW (Underwater Archaeological Wing) in 2001.

Long-term studies have been going on at Dwarka, which is submerged underwater off the Gujarat coast. The seabed around port towns like Poompuhar, that is mentioned in Tamil history, and at Mahabalipuram are being studied. Sophisticated sonar equipment is used to track and trace well-known shipwrecks within India's territorial waters. The idea is not to lift them, but to study them in their current state. Advanced diving gear allows archaeologists to investigate underwater sites and take extensive photographs for later study.

The Konkan coast was known for piracy. Here pirates waited to attack Mughal-era ships that carried pilgrims to the Haj. Local pirates attacked English, Portuguese or Dutch ships and English pirates attacked everyone. So there must be a lot of treasure lying in the Arabian Sea that private firms would love to 'find and keep'!

On 2 November 2001, at the UNESCO general assembly, member nations signed a treaty called the UNESCO Convention on Underwater Cultural Heritage. It protects all sunken ships, submerged cities or sites, etc., of over 100 years. The aim is to maintain underwater sites as is, for future generations to study and reveal more about our history.

'And what's this?' Nina asked, picking up the magazine Apu had left carelessly on the table. The masthead proclaimed *History Hunters* and in small type, 'Junior' below it.

'Hey, this looks cool,' she said.

Apu laughed, 'I thought you just said you'd had enough of history!'

Nina stuck her tongue out at him and turned to the page that had the school's bookmark in it. And she gasped in shock.

There, across two spreads, was their story, 'Nobel Laureates and Whispering Galleries'! And below it, their names!

They stared at each other in shock. Was it Mathur Sir or Principal Ma'am who'd sent off their assignment, they wondered. They looked up to find the librarian had joined them at their table.

'So what do you think about that?' she asked with a twinkle in her eye.

'Ma'am, tell us who sent it to the magazine… Ma'am…please,' Nina begged. But the librarian had walked away, saying over her shoulder, 'I have no idea…why don't you ask Mathur Sir?' leaving Apu and Nina completely mystified, though thrilled to see their names in print.

Apu swiped the magazine out of a still-dazed Nina's hands, and peered at both their names below the title. And because he was a bit irritated that something Nina had researched had been sent to the magazine, he wickedly pointed out, 'Must be so irritating to have done all the research for this article, but have my name appear before yours, right?'

Nina hadn't noticed that, so she walked across to check. Yes, it did infuriate her, now that this had been pointed out. But she spotted something else that made her smile.

Taking the magazine from Apu, she sat down to read, saying, 'At least they didn't spell my name wrong! Wonder if anyone in class will notice that Apu Raghavan has been renamed Abu Raghan? Maybe I should tell them!'

'Don't you dare!' Apu snapped, making a grab for the magazine, again. The librarian turned around just as the brand new copy she'd just handed to them ripped down the spine as they pulled it in opposite directions.

She sighed. 'They'll soon be back here,' she concluded. 'Kids like this will spend half their school life in detention.'